ST. PATRICK AND HIS WORLD

St. Patrick and His World

MIKE AQUILINA

Scepter

Copyright © 2024, Michael Aquilina

The total or partial reproduction of this book is not permitted, nor its informatic treatment, or the transmission of any form or by any means, either electronic, mechanic, photocopy, or other methods without the prior written permission of the owners of the copyright.

Unless otherwise noted, Scripture texts from the New and Old Testaments are taken from The Holy Bible Revised Standard Version Catholic Edition © 1965 and 1966 by the Division of Christian Education of the National Council of the Churches of Christ in the United States. All rights reserved. All copyrighted material is used by permission of the copyright owner. No part of it may be reproduced without permission in writing from the copyright owner.

Some quoted material in this book is drawn from centuries-old translations. The author has sometimes adapted this material for easier comprehension by modern readers. Latin originals, when available, have been referenced and compared.

Published by Scepter Publishers, Inc.
info@scepterpublishers.org
www.scepterpublishers.org
800-322-8773
New York

All rights reserved.

Cover design: Studio Red Design
Text design and pagination: Studio Red Design

Library of Congress Control Number: 2023940575

ISBN
Paperback: 978-1-59417-504-6
eBook: 978-1-59417-505-3

Printed in the United States of America

Contents

Prologue 1

Introduction 5

What We Know 7

Growing up in Britain 15

The Ends of the Earth 31

The Escape 41

Preparing for the Mission (Patrick and His Sources) ... 56

Patrick and His Prayer 71

Patrick and His Work 86

The Conversion of Ireland 105

Patrick and His Legacy 134

Sources 140

Prologue

As a Catholic Irishman I thank God for a book about St. Patrick that distinguishes between fact and legend, expertly presenting the historical evidence without inexpertly dismissing legend as a possible source of truth. We know from historical evidence, for example, that Patrick was traumatically snatched as a sixteen-year-old boy from his own people on the English coast by the pirates of Niall of the Nine Hostages. Niall had become High King of all Ireland on the night that he kidnapped the firstborn sons of his nine main rivals and forced them to submit to him under the threat of execution of their sons.

We also know that a direct descendant and heir to the throne of King Niall later became a Christian in response to the evangelization of Patrick's disciples, and then a monk, and then a saint: St. Colmcille (variations include Colum or Columba) of Derry, Ireland, and then Iona, Scotland, evangelizer of the Scottish (the Picts) and the English (the Angles and Saxons). St. Colum's conversion had a huge social impact in the Ireland of his time. Many followed him into the Church's embrace. Patrick, the kidnapped slave and Ireland's patron saint, was the converting link between the tyrant and the heir, and the miraculous conversion of a nation. God's vengeance is sweet.

St. Patrick played his part in God's plan for Anglo-Irish relations. He was tormented by a recurring nightmare. The very people who robbed him of his youth and freedom begged him to return to them with the Good News. Their animalized faces appeared to him over and over again, night after night, in haunted sleep. This is not legend, it's historical fact; we know it from his own personal testimony, which has the ring of raw truth about it even while sounding like the stuff of which legends are made.

The historical and legendary dimensions of truly great men are often difficult to distinguish. According to one St. Patrick legend, for example, after initial failures in his missionary activity, he climbed Ireland's sacred mountain, Croagh Patrick, to spend forty days and forty nights of prayer and penance on its summit, beseeching God to grant him the blessing of being the Abraham of Ireland with a multitude of descendants as numerous as the stars of the sky and the sands of the seashore. According to the legend, his prayers were answered.

Historical fact? We have no way of knowing. Maybe not. But that doesn't mean there is no element of truth to the story. It reflects the spirit and the life story of the saint in a way that is corroborated by the historical evidence. If it happened, it wouldn't have been St. Patrick's first mountaintop experience, as the saint himself has told us, and as Mike Aquilina describes in the following pages.

Aquilina also mentions the interesting fact that St. Patrick and St. Augustine were contemporaries. Augustine was born some thirty years before Patrick, and Patrick died some thirty years after Augustine: they coincided for some forty-five years on this storm-tossed planet of ours. Augustine is a famous witness of the collapse of one civilization, and Patrick is the famous protagonist of the rise of another civilization: he set in motion the movement that produced the re-evangelizers and rebuilders of Christian Europe. Two men so different and yet so united as witnesses to the crucified and risen Christ. Little did Augustine realize that a solitary man in a far-flung island was planting the seeds of the renewal of the civilization whose passing he mourned. They are surely swapping stories in heaven as we speak. What a fascinating tradition we Catholics have!

May God grant us, through the intercession of St. Patrick, the grace to be haunted benevolently, night and day, by the anguished faces of our neo-pagan contemporaries in Ireland and throughout the whole world, who unwittingly crave the Good News to be rescued from a wretched slavery and introduced to the horizons of eternal life and love and meaning. May this book awaken in our hearts the redemptive longings of the Heart of Christ and the heart of St. Patrick. Thank you, Mike, for communicating to us his life and his spirit. May we repay you with our apostolic zeal.

Fr. Colum Power, SHM

CHAPTER 1

Introduction

St. Patrick is a man perhaps more beloved, revered, and celebrated than any other Father of the Church.

And yet he is rarely listed among the Fathers. I never counted him among the Fathers of the Church myself. I certainly knew him as a great saint, but Father of the Church? He just wasn't on the list.

But then I got COVID.

Luckily, it was very mild for me. And luckily, at the same time, I received a doctoral dissertation by Fr. William Swan, a priest in Ireland. I spent my week of COVID reading his dissertation in bed. And by the end of it, I was persuaded that St. Patrick of Ireland deserves to be numbered among the Fathers of the Church.

Everybody knows St. Patrick. He's ubiquitous in popular culture. He is the patron saint of Ireland—and patron to the enormous Irish diaspora worldwide. Every year, millions celebrate his feast day, March 17, with parades and pub crawls and green beer.

He is the stuff of many legends. People who don't know the gospel know that the mythological Patrick drove the snakes out of Ireland—and that he used a shamrock to explain the Trinity. But these legends arise only in later folklore and seem to have no basis in historical fact.

What we know for sure about Patrick is what we find in the two pieces of writing that are indisputably his—his *Confession* and his "Letter to the Soldiers of Coroticus."

These tell us much about his inner life—his emotional and spiritual life. And they tell us much about his historical circumstances and his ministry. Yet they are often dismissed because of their rough, rude, pidgin Latin. They stand in stark contrast with the refined works of Augustine, Chrysostom, and even Vincent of Lérins. But their effects and influence in Christian history and culture have arguably been as great as, or greater than, the masterpieces of eloquence produced by those men.

So let's take a look at the life that produced those works. Let's start with what we know about St. Patrick.

CHAPTER 2
What We Know

First of all, St. Patrick didn't banish the snakes from Ireland. We know that for a fact. Pliny the Elder, who wrote a giant encyclopedia of world knowledge (and died getting a closer look at the eruption of Mount Vesuvius in AD 79), mentioned as a fun fact about Ireland that there were no snakes in the island. That was three centuries or so before Patrick was born. And if that's not enough, modern paleontologists have gone through the fossil record with a fine-toothed comb. Their verdict: no evidence of snakes in Ireland.

Actually, the first time the story of a saint banishing the snakes from Ireland comes up in literature, the saint isn't Patrick. It's St. Columba. Not until about 1200 do we find the story associated with St. Patrick.

So we can start the story of Patrick with one definite fact: he didn't banish the snakes from Ireland.

This turns out to be one of the few facts we know for certain about Patrick that Patrick didn't tell us himself.

In some ways, we know very little about St. Patrick. We don't even know when he was born, when he came to Ireland, or when he died. Various sources give us all those dates, but they give us different dates.

In another way, though, we know everything that's really important about St. Patrick. We know him from the inside—how he thought and how he felt. We know him because he put his heart and soul into his own writings. Those writings are a terrible frustration for historians, because Patrick never mentions dates and doesn't see the point of sticking to a chronological order. But for those of us who want to know the inner heart of a saint, the whole man is there in what he wrote.

From his own writings we have the main outlines of his life, although there are big gaps, and it's not always easy to tell what the order of events was. Much more importantly, though, we know his personality. We know what Patrick the man was like.

Two Letters from His Own Hand

Patrick wrote two things that everybody agrees are his. One is the little book known as the *Confession*, and the other is the "Letter to the Soldiers of Coroticus." Everyone agrees that they must be authentic, partly because they're so badly written. The Latin is difficult and ungrammatical; sentences break off or lose their way; and the stories are often hard to follow and seldom complete. If you told Patrick he was a bad writer, he would certainly agree. "And so to-day I blush and am exceedingly afraid to lay bare my lack of education; because I am unable to make my meaning plain in a few words to the learned,"[1] he tells us in one of his many apologies for his poor style.

But his poor style is exactly why we know him so well. Patrick seems to have written exactly the way he would talk—in the Vulgar Latin that was already on its way to becoming Portuguese, Spanish, French, Italian, Romanian, and the rest of the Romance languages. And not just the way he would talk in everyday life, but the way he would talk when he was really wrought up about something, as he was when he wrote both the *Confession* and the "Letter." This is how we know we're encountering the real Patrick.

---

1. St. Patrick, *Confession*, 10, as quoted in *St. Patrick: His Writings and Life*, ed. and trans. Newport J. D. White (London: Society for Promoting Christian Knowledge, 1920), p. 34.

If these two documents had been later forgeries, or if they had been substantially altered, someone would certainly have cleaned up the Latin. Later forgers would also not have put in so many declarations of the writer's inadequacy and sinfulness—only a saint would do that.[2]

Both of these writings give us Patrick at a vulnerable moment, when his emotions are stirred up and he is probably not thinking as clearly as he would like.

The *Confession* is a very brief life story, written to answer some criticisms of Patrick's ministry in Ireland. Apparently, some people had accused him of profiteering using his position as bishop and evangelist. We don't know exactly what the charges were, but refuting them leads Patrick to describe his work in some detail.

The "Letter to the Soldiers of Coroticus" was written after a British warlord's raiding party had killed some of Patrick's newly converted flock and taken some others off to be sold as slaves. Patrick was understandably upset when he wrote it, and because he was so worked up, he reveals a lot of his personality. He also mentions a few facts about his own life and work that he didn't cover in the *Confession*.

---

2. William Declan Swan, "The Experience of God in the Writings of St. Patrick: Reworking a Faith Received" (PhD diss., Pontificia Università Gregoriana, 2012), pp. 44–45.

Since Patrick wasn't writing for historians when he wrote these documents, he doesn't give historians the information they would like to have. It would have pleased historians if Patrick had written down dates, or even just one date. But he didn't. It would have pleased historians if Patrick had given them more names to work with, but he gives them almost none. He does give us one important name: the British warlord Coroticus. But there was more than one Coroticus, and historians have never managed to agree on which one Patrick meant.

We also wish he had given us more details about Ireland—where he went, what he saw there, what life was like. As far as historians know, there is precisely one person who saw Ireland in the 400s, wrote something about it, and left us a record that has survived to the present day. That one person is St. Patrick. He is our only eyewitness to fifth-century Ireland. But he isn't writing a travel guide to the island, so he doesn't give us much to go on.

The Other Sources

All the other chronicles, histories, and biographies that speak of the 400s in Ireland were written later, after all the people who lived through that time were dead. Those later chronicles and histories may have relied on things that were written down in the 400s—documents that have since been lost to history. But they are secondary sources at best, and we can't rely on them the way we rely on St. Patrick's own writings.

Still, we can't dismiss them altogether. Oral tradition in preliterate societies can be surprisingly accurate. A literate society like ours comes to rely on writing so much that we lose the ability to remember things and to pass them along to each generation. As a result, we assume that it's impossible. But in a mostly illiterate society, much of the intellectual activity is devoted to precisely that: learning traditions by heart, repeating them over and over, and teaching young people to do the same thing, so that they can hand down the most important stories, facts, laws, and rules of etiquette to their children and grandchildren.

So we'll find a lot of stories about Patrick in a kind of middle ground. We can't rely on them as historical facts, but we can't dismiss them the way we dismissed the story of the snakes. We can try to figure out how plausible they are, but in the end, the best we can say is that some of them are more likely to be true than false, and some are more likely to be false than true.

With St. Patrick, it's even harder to sort out what's true than with many other historical figures. As we'll see later on, more than one historian has argued that there was more than one Patrick. If stories of two separate evangelists have been combined into one, it would explain why the St. Patrick of legend lived to the age of 120. And some of the chronicles seem to suggest more than one Patrick. There are murky references to a shadowy "Old-Patrick" who was not the important one, and some references to a "younger Patrick" who lived after the great St. Patrick.[3]

Outline of a Life

So here is the bare outline of Patrick's life as he himself tells it:

1. He was born in Britain, and thus considered himself a Roman citizen.
2. He was raised in a wealthy family of Christian clergy, but he had no serious Christian faith of his own.
3. At the age of sixteen, he was kidnapped by Irish raiders, along with many other British people, and sold as a slave.

---

3. D. A. Binchy, "Patrick and His Biographers: Ancient and Modern," *Studia Hibernica* 2, 1962: 7–173, pp. 115ff.

4. He escaped slavery after six years, but he was called back to Ireland by repeated dreams.
5. He became a bishop whose mission was the conversion of the Irish.
6. He was quite successful, possibly because it was part of his method to be absolutely trustworthy.
7. At some time, he lost a large number of new converts to a raiding party from the British warlord Coroticus.
8. At some other time, he was accused of some sort of mishandling of his mission to Ireland.

This is the outline of his life as we can gather it from Patrick's own writings. Much of the rest of what is told about Patrick is legend: it might be true, and it might not be.

But we do know some things about the world Patrick lived in, and that will tell us some more about what Patrick's life must have been like. Let's start with where he was born: the remote Roman province of Britain.

CHAPTER 3

Growing up in Britain

Patrick was born a Roman citizen in Britain. We know exactly where he was born, because he tells us himself: it was in the village of Banavem Taberniae. Unfortunately, we don't know exactly where Banavem Taberniae was. The best we can say is that it was in the northwestern part of what is called England today, near Carlisle—unless it was somewhere else. No one has succeeded in identifying Banavem Taberniae. Or, to put it another way, far too many people have succeeded in identifying Banavem Taberniae, and they all disagree.[4]

But we do know a good bit about what life was like for young Patrick. His parents gave him a good Latin name: Patricius, which means "noble" (it's the word that gives us *patrician*). He was a Roman and he was well off, and that meant the same thing the length and breadth of the Empire.

Born a Roman

All freeborn people in the Roman Empire were Roman citizens by the time Patrick was born, even way up in Britain. Patrick was as much a citizen of Rome as a child born in Fairbanks, Alaska, is a citizen of the United States. And Britain was as Roman as Alaska is American: it had its own local culture, but the towns and suburban villas looked like towns and villas in every other province of the Empire. Most of the better-off citizens were probably bilingual, speaking both British (the ancestor of today's Welsh and Breton) and Vulgar Latin, the common language of the western half of the Roman Empire. This isn't certain:

---

4. Even the name is disputed; some scholars correct the manuscripts to read, "Banna Venta Berniae," which they still can't find. Charles Thomas, *Britain and Ireland in Early Christian Times, AD 400–800* (London: Thames and Hudson, 1971), p. 83.

what Patrick himself says about it is ambiguous. In one place, writing in Latin, he says,

> For my speech and language is translated into a tongue not my own, as can be easily proved from the savour of my writing, in what fashion I have been taught and am learned in speech.[5]

Here he is apologizing for his lack of education; the words might mean that Latin is a foreign language to him, but many commentators have taken them to mean that he has spent so many years speaking a foreign language—Irish—that his Latin is rusty. He makes grammatical mistakes in Latin, but they are the kind of common grammatical mistakes by which uneducated speakers ultimately turned Latin into the Romance languages. It seems most likely, then, that Patrick grew up using everyday Latin regularly, but never got the education that would have transformed the language of the market stalls into the language of Cicero and Jerome.

He probably would have had that education if his life had gone the way it was supposed to go. Patrick was better off than many of the citizens in Britain. His father was a

---

5. St. Patrick, *Confession*, 9, as quoted in White, p. 33.

decurion named Calpurnius, a wealthy landowner who was also part of the hereditary town council.

Being a decurion gave a Roman citizen one unwelcome burden: he was responsible for the taxes in his area. It was a difficulty made more difficult by the fact that the very rich—the senatorial class—didn't pay taxes at all. Taxes were owed by the landowners who weren't rich enough to be senators, and it was the decurions' job to collect that tax. Whatever they couldn't collect from lesser landowners, they had to pay out of their own pockets. This was an obviously flawed system, but the only emperor who ever tackled it head-on was Julian, who tried to make the richest of the rich pay taxes. He died young on a misguided expedition into Persia—and because he had deserted Christianity for the old pagan religion, he was remembered forever as Julian the Apostate. No other emperor wanted to be associated with the Apostate's ideas, so tax reform never happened.

We can easily understand why many of the decurions tried to wiggle out from under this burden by any means possible. If they got rich enough, they could buy their way into the senatorial class. If they got desperate enough, they could give up their property; some even sold themselves as slaves.

In other words, everything fell on the middle class, which continually shrank as more and more of them found some way out from under the burden. Since it was unthinkable that the very rich should be forced to pay taxes, the only way the imperial government could come up with to keep the tax money flowing was to make more and more restrictive laws designed to keep the decurions in their place. The laws got more desperately restrictive as the decurial class shrank, and the decurial class shrank even more as the laws got more restrictive.

A Clerical Family

One way out for some decurions was to enter the Church, although the imperial laws tried to close off that loophole more than once. Patrick's family seems to have made the Church the family business. His father Calpurnius was a deacon, and Calpurnius' father before him was a priest. (Priestly celibacy was not yet a universal rule in the West in those days.)

This does not necessarily mean that they were enthusiastically religious. By this time, Christianity had been the official religion of the Roman Empire for a while. Working for the Church was a good career, and a good way of avoiding the responsibilities of secular life. Many priests and deacons were certainly committed Christians, but there were others who, while they were certainly Christian, took the position more as a job than as a vocation.

This may explain some of the little Patrick tells us about his youth. We know that Patrick's father was well off: he had a number of "menservants and maidservants" on his property.[6] So Patrick grew up in a family that had some considerable property, and one that had been Christian for at least two generations before him. Yet he tells us himself that he was not living as a Christian. "I did not believe in the living God, nor had I since my infancy," he says.[7] He doesn't mean he was a pagan. He had certainly gone to church, but like many young people, he didn't take it seriously: "[W]e departed away from God, and kept not his commandments, and were not obedient to our priests, who used to admonish us for our salvation."[8]

So he had heard the homilies, but he didn't get much out of them. Typical teenager.

Since he says, "[W]e departed away from God," however, he might mean something more than not caring much about religion Monday through Saturday. The Pelagian heresy may have been popular in Britain when

---

6. St. Patrick, "Letter to Coroticus," 10, as quoted in White, p. 56.
7. St. Patrick, *Confession*, 27, as quoted in White, p. 40.
8. St. Patrick, *Confession*, 1, as quoted in White, p. 31.

Patrick was growing up; it's possible that he means he and many of his neighbors fell away from the Catholic Church into heresy. (We'll hear more about Pelagius and his heresy later.) We might be more confident if we knew when Patrick was born, but he doesn't give dates. He didn't need to give any dates: he was writing to people who knew who he was and how old he was.

Patrick isn't interested in giving details of his youth at all—unlike St. Augustine, he isn't trying to psychoanalyze himself. Only one incident stands out. At some point in his young life, when he was about fifteen years old, Patrick committed a sin that haunted him for the rest of his life. What was it? He doesn't say—not because he was too embarrassed to mention it, but because the people he was writing to already knew all about it.

That's all we know until Patrick was about sixteen years old. Then his comfortable Roman life suddenly came to an end. He became a tiny piece of collateral damage in the decline and fall of the Roman Empire.

The Decline and Fall of Roman Britain

If he had stayed in Britain, Patrick would probably have been finishing up his education. He would probably have studied rhetoric, to give him a suitable polish to fit him either for his position as a decurion or for a place in the Church.

"Bilingualism was normal among the educated part of the British population," says the Latin scholar Christine Mohrmann.[9] Since Patrick speaks of Latin as "our" language, it's likely he spoke some of it at home. Philologists who study these things have pointed out that the Latin loanwords that seeped into the British language (the language that became Welsh) are everyday words, not scholarly terms, and that means Vulgar Latin—the ordinary spoken Latin of ordinary people—was common in Britain.[10] The "backwoods" and "untaught" (*rusticissima* and *indoctus*) Latin Patrick wrote in later life would have been the ordinary language he grew up speaking. He would have spent his late youth and early adulthood polishing that Latin into a literary language suitable for showing off. But he never got the chance, because Britain wasn't the place it used to be.

9. Christine Mohrmann, *The Latin of St. Patrick*, as quoted in Binchy, p. 23.
10. Kenneth Jackson, *Language and History in Early Britain*, (Edinburgh: University Press, 1953), p. 80. "That the great mass, if not practically the whole, were borrowed from spoken Latin is a point which needs to be stressed. These are for the most part not 'learned' loans from book Latin and written sources, but popular borrowings from the living Latin language used in Roman Britain." Binchy (p. 24) cites this as evidence that Patrick grew up speaking Latin, and that the Latin he ended up writing was the Latin he grew up with. Not everyone agrees with this, however, and some historians think Patrick spoke only British until he entered the Church.

For a long time, Britain had been a safe and prosperous province. But it was surrounded on all sides by "barbarians"—non-Roman people who wouldn't mind having a bit of that prosperity for themselves. When the Empire was strong, there were solid legions to defend the territory, and those barbarians had to stay on the outside and grumble. But as the Empire weakened, and invaders threatened Rome itself, more and more of the defenses were pulled back from Britain, and the barbarians took note. When Rome itself was sacked by Goths in the year 410, the imperial government had more pressing problems on its plate than the distant province of Britain.

Much of the decline could be attributed to one man—the emperor Honorius, probably the most disastrous emperor the Roman Empire ever had.

When Theodosius the Great died in 395, his empire was divided between his two sons, Arcadius in the East and Honorius in the West. No one knew it at the time, but Theodosius would turn out to be the last emperor ever to hold power over the entire Roman Empire at once. Honorius was ten years old when he inherited absolute power over the Western Empire. That didn't give him much time for character development.

The famous historian Thomas Hodgkin described Honorius as a kind of vacancy in history.

> It is impossible to imagine a character more utterly destitute of moral colour, of self-determining energy, than that of the younger son of Theodosius. In Arcadius we do at length discover traces of uxoriousness, a blemish in some rulers, but which becomes almost a merit in him when contrasted with the absolute vacancy, the inability to love, to hate, to think, to execute, almost to be, which marks the impersonal personality of Honorius.[11]

While Honorius cowered in easily defended Ravenna, on the swampy coast of Italy and off the track of any invaders, Germanic hordes rampaged across the Western Empire. Once in a while, a competent general would rise up and stop the barbarians for a while. But Honorius was more afraid of competent Roman generals than he was of barbarians, and the competent general would always end up losing his head.

Britain did not fall from its prosperity all at once. It had a long century or two of ups and downs. But the general trend was downward, as far as the Romanized Britons were

---

11. Thomas Hodgkin, *Italy and Her Invaders* in *The Visigothic Invasion* (Oxford: Clarendon Press, 1892), 1:643.

concerned. Looking back from some time in the 500s, the British writer Gildas the Wise (ca. 516-570) wrote a screed *On the Ruin of Britain*: "[T]he subject of my complaint is the general destruction of everything that is good, and the general growth of evil throughout the land," he tells us at the beginning,[12] which doesn't leave us in doubt about where he stands.

Politics was part of the problem. One of Britain's main exports was pretenders to the imperial throne. It seemed as if every few years, some general was proclaimed emperor in Britain and went off to conquer the Empire. They almost all failed, but they all had in mind the example of the one who had spectacularly succeeded: Constantine, the first Christian emperor, who was proclaimed emperor in York.

It may be that the British, or the soldiers stationed in Britain, thought the central government wasn't doing enough to protect them, and went looking every few years for someone who would do the job. That was the wrong solution, because of course, the first thing an imperial pretender had to do was take an army with him from Britain toward Rome.

---

12. Gildas Sapiens, *De Excidio et Conquestu Britanniae* §1, in Gildas Sapiens and Nennius, *The Works of Gildas and Nennius*, trans. J. A. Giles (London: James Bohn, 1941), p. 1.

One of the most successful was Magnus Maximus, who actually did get himself recognized as emperor in Britain and Gaul for a while, before he was defeated by Theodosius the Great in 388. Gildas sees his ambition as one of the great disasters in British history. Maximus took all the soldiers with him, leaving Britain to be overrun by barbarians.

After this, Britain is deprived of all her soldiery and armed bands, of her cruel governors, and of the flower of her youth, who went with Maximus but never returned. Utterly ignorant of the art of war, Britain groaned in amazement for many years under the cruelty of two foreign nations—the Scots from the northwest, and the Picts from the north.[13]

The Picts were the native people of what is now Scotland. The Scots were the Irish, who had not yet overrun Scotland and named it after themselves.

After these disasters, it was clear that Britain was no longer the safe and peaceful place it had been through more than three centuries of Roman control. When the rebel emperor Constantine III took over much of the West from the useless emperor Honorius, the barbarians took advantage of the instability and poured across the

13. Gildas, as quoted in Gildas and Nennius, 14:13.

landscape into all the provinces. Constantine seemed unable to do anything about it. The pagan historians tell us that the Britons were forced to take things into their own hands.

> Constantine being unable to withstand these, the greater part of the army being in Spain, the barbarians beyond the Rhine made such unbounded incursions over every province, as to reduce not only the Britons, but some of the Celtic nations also to the necessity of revolting from the empire, and living no longer under the Roman laws but as they themselves pleased. The Britons therefore took up arms, and incurred many dangerous enterprises for their own protection, until they had freed their cities from the barbarians who besieged them. In a similar manner, the whole of Armorica, with other provinces of Gaul, delivered themselves by the same means: expelling the Roman magistrates or officers, and erecting a government, such as they pleased, of their own.
>
> Thus happened this revolt or defection of Britain and the Celtic nations, when Constantine usurped the empire, by whose negligent

> government the barbarians were emboldened to commit such devastations.[14]

This rebellion probably seemed like a temporary measure to the British. They would have expected that, when the two imperial idiots vying for the throne had killed each other, order would be restored and Rome would be great again. It had happened many times before, and there was no reason to suppose it wouldn't happen now. The British still thought of themselves as Romans for a long time afterwards.[15] They had no way of knowing that they had actually seen the last of the Roman government in their island.

Honorius, though, managed to hold on to power for eighteen years. As St. Patrick's biographer R. P. C. Hanson puts it,

> But though Honorius was quite incapable himself of preventing the Western Roman Empire dissolving before the assaults of barbarians, he had an amazing capacity for ensuring that he, and only he, should preside over its dissolution.[16]

---

14. Zosimus, *New History*, as quoted in *The History of Count Zosimus* (London: J. Davis, 1814), 6: 174-175.
15. R. P. C. Hanson, *Saint Patrick: His Origins and Career* (Oxford: Clarendon Press, 1968), p. 11.
16. Hanson, p. 7.

He managed to defeat every would-be usurper—eight of them, depending on how you count—and then went back to ignoring the barbarians. The ancient historian Procopius tells the story—which may or may not be a malicious rumor—of Honorius' reaction to the sack of Rome in 410: he had a fancy rooster named Rome, and when someone burst in to tell him "Rome is destroyed!" the emperor answered, "What? But he was just eating out of my hand moments ago!" He was very relieved to hear that it was only Rome the city that had been destroyed. This tale may not be true, but it certainly tells us what Romans thought of Honorius.[17]

Naturally, Honorius had little interest in defending far-off Britain when he couldn't even defend Rome. When the British sent a message begging for help, he told them to take care of their own defense and stop bothering him.

Slowly, then, the government in Britain degenerated from the orderly Roman provincial system into a set of squabbling kingdoms. Individual warlords controlled as much territory as they could grab, and when they weren't fighting the barbarians, they were fighting each other. Naturally, power tended to accumulate in the hands of

---

17. Procopius, *History of the Wars*, trans. H. B. Dewing (Cambridge, MA: Harvard University Press, 1914), 3.2:25–26.

the most ruthless. We'll see how this change broke into Patrick's life much later on in a very dramatic way.

Walls rose around the peaceful towns and cities. Lookout towers went up along the coasts. But the barbarians outside knew that Roman strength wasn't what it used to be. If they came suddenly and in sufficient numbers, they could carry off what they wanted before anybody stopped them.

And that was what happened to Patrick.

When Patrick was sixteen, raiders from Ireland suddenly appeared and fell on his father's farm. They "made havoc of the menservants and maidservants of my father's house."[18] It must have been a large force: "I went into captivity to Ireland with many thousands of persons," Patrick says.

Why did they carry off so many captives? Because human beings were the most valuable livestock of all. Patrick was sold as a slave.

---

18. St. Patrick, "Letter," 10, as quoted in White, p. 56.

CHAPTER 4

The Ends of the Earth

For a Roman like Patrick, Ireland was *outside*. It was outside the Roman Empire and outside Christendom. It was practically outside the world.

Romans tended to see civilization and the Roman Empire as the same thing. The extent of the Roman Empire was the extent of civilization. It was a little different in the East, where there were ancient, civilized empires on the borders, like Persia and Ethiopia. But in western Europe, whatever was not Roman was merely barbarian.

So, when Patrick tells us that he and thousands of others were abducted from Britain by Irish pirates, he sees it as going to the farthest boundaries of the world. "And the Lord *poured upon* us *the fury of his anger*, and scattered us amongst many heathen, even *unto the ends of the earth*, where now my littleness may be seen amongst men of another nation."[19]

Nothing Familiar

It was a place where nothing was familiar—at least at first. Even the language was incomprehensible to him: "I went into captivity in language," as he describes it.[20] The Irish spoke a Celtic language, but it was as different from Patrick's British as German is from English. And Latin, the universal language in the Western Empire, wouldn't do him any good in Ireland.

The culture was completely different, too. The Roman Empire had conquered out to the limits of what was practical to conquer. Thus, the Empire had absorbed almost everything in the known world that was civilized (except in the East, where a couple of strong empires balanced the Roman Empire), and civilization had become,

---

19. St. Patrick, *Confession*, 1, as quoted in White, p. 31, emphasis in original.
20. St. Patrick, *Confession*, 10, as quoted in White, p. 34.

practically speaking, one giant nation. In Patrick's time, it was usually ruled by two emperors, one in the East at Constantinople and one in the West at Milan or Ravenna. Often those two emperors disagreed; frequently they were fighting. But in general, the Empire was open from one end to the other, and a Roman could travel from Britain to Palestine without crossing a national border.

That was a huge advantage when the Christians started to spread the Gospel. Ships were constantly going from here to there, and soldiers were always being moved from the west to the east, or the south to the north, and a Roman with some ambition who wasn't getting anywhere in one province might pick up and move to Palestine or Britain. Travel was easy and common, and Christians traveled as much as anyone else. The Gospel spread quickly, even when it was illegal to be a Christian.

But all that stopped at the borders of the Empire. There was plenty of trade with other nations, but nothing like the easy travel from here to there that took place inside the Empire. The result was that Christianity grew very quickly inside the Empire, and much more slowly in most places outside. When Constantine made Christianity the favored religion of the Empire, Rome became a Christian nation surrounded by pagan nations.[21] The power and prestige of Rome made Christianity attractive to those pagan barbarians, but most of the nations on the periphery of the Empire were still pagan in Patrick's time.

Ireland was one of them.

Ireland the Unknown

When it comes to Ireland during St. Patrick's time, there's very little to know. There are traditional stories, and there are dated entries in chronicles that were written much later. But when we try to pin down any particular incident or fact, it evaporates into mist. Almost everything that purports to be a history of that time was written down much later. In fact, there are only two writings in all of history that describe Ireland in the 400s from the point of view of a known eyewitness—and they're both by St. Patrick.[22]

What we do know was that Ireland was organized very differently from the Roman Empire. Ireland in the 400s had more than a hundred little kingdoms.[23] We don't know exactly how those kingdoms related to each other back then, but in later ages, the kingdoms were loosely

---

21. There were significant exceptions. Armenia, for example, was officially Christian before Rome was.
22. Roy Flechner, *Saint Patrick Retold: The Legend and History of Ireland's Patron Saint* (Princeton: Princeton University Press, 2019), p. 95.
23. Binchy, 148.

knit into a cascading hierarchy, with little kings reluctantly submitting to the loose authority of bigger regional kings, and the bigger regional kings all supposedly owing allegiance to one "high king." In practice, they were all fighting each other most of the time. The hierarchy might not have been so clearly organized in Patrick's time, but we can probably take it for granted that the part about fighting most of the time was true.

So Ireland was a different world from what Patrick was used to. But it wasn't a completely unknown world. It was not part of the Roman Empire, but Roman trade reached everywhere. Romans spiced their food with pepper from India. Rich Roman ladies wore silk from China. Ireland, too, had things of value to the Romans. Roman coins have been found in various places on the island, some dating back to the time of the Republic, before the first emperor. Even in the time of Tacitus, more than three centuries before Patrick was born, Ireland was familiar to Roman merchants. It seems to have been a regular stop on the route from Spain to Britain, since Tacitus imagines it as "just between Britain and Spain." He adds that "its ports and landings are better known" than Britain's, "through the frequency of commerce and merchants."[24] Of course, after Tacitus' time, Britain became a thoroughly Romanized province, but it had just been conquered when Tacitus wrote. He could not see why the Romans had not conquered Ireland as well. One of the petty kings of Ireland, "expelled by domestic dissension," had told him "that with a single legion and a few auxiliaries, Ireland might be conquered and preserved." But for whatever reason, the Romans never made the attempt.

It might have been because the culture in Ireland was very different from Britain's. Britain and Gaul shared a mutually intelligible Celtic language and religion, and were probably even integrated politically to some degree. If Gaul was conquered but Britain was not, then Britain would be a constant source of agitation against Roman rule. To hold on to Gaul, it was almost a requirement to conquer Britain, too. But Ireland didn't pose the same problem.

So Ireland, especially around the coast that faced the continent, had experience with Roman merchants bringing Roman ideas. One of those ideas would certainly have been Christianity. When Patrick was abducted and

---

24. Cornelius Tacitus, *Agricola*, 24, as quoted in *The Works of Tacitus*, trans. Thomas Gordon (London: J. and F. Rivington, 1770), 4:93.

taken to Ireland, there were probably already groups of Christians there.

But they weren't numerous where Patrick ended up. If there were any at all, he doesn't seem to have noticed them. As far as Patrick was concerned, he had been hauled outside Christendom to a land of heathens.

And that was where he learned to be a real Christian.

A Slave's Life

Patrick was sold to a master who put him to work tending the flocks (of sheep or whatever other animals the man had). He seems to have ended up somewhere in the Wood of Foclut or Fochlath, which was probably in the far west of the island—"by the western sea" is how Patrick describes it.[25] The aristocrat's son had to stay out in the Irish weather, which is not always perfectly pleasant. The conditions were brutal, with little accommodation for the cold, wet climate. Yet in his *Confession*, he doesn't complain. He recognizes that he is one of thousands of British forcibly enslaved by pirates, many of them lukewarm Christians like Patrick.

But the good part was that he had a lot of time to himself. As he stood out in the cold and wind, he started

---

25. St. Patrick, *Confession*, 23, as quoted in John Healy, *The Life and Writings of St. Patrick* (Dublin: M. H. Gill & Son, 1905), p. 65.

to think. He remembered all the lessons he had tried to ignore in his childhood.

> And there the Lord *opened the understanding* of my unbelief that, even though late, I might call my faults to remembrance, and that I might *turn with all my heart* to the Lord my God, who *regarded* my *low estate* and pitied the youth of my ignorance, and kept me before I knew him, and before I had discernment or could distinguish between good and evil, and protected me and comforted me as a father does his son.[26]

Once Patrick had started to think over the lessons he had learned when he was younger, he started to do something he probably hadn't done in a long time. He started to pray.

Getting to Know God

As he prayed, Patrick began to undergo a deep conversion. He recognized the sins of his former life, and he was grateful to God for the opportunity to detach himself from them. He saw his present difficulties as a blessing.

> Now, after I came to Ireland, tending flocks was my daily occupation; and constantly I used to pray

---

26. St. Patrick, *Confession*, 2, as quoted in White, pp. 31–32.

in the day time. Love of God and the fear of him increased more and more, and faith grew, and the spirit was moved, so that in one day [I would say] as many as a hundred prayers, and at night nearly as many, so that I used to stay even in the woods and on the mountain [to this end]. And before daybreak I used to be roused to prayer, in snow, in frost, in rain; and I felt no hurt; nor was there any sluggishness in me—as I now see, because then *the spirit was fervent* within me.[27]

Six years passed this way. Patrick developed a deep intimacy with God the Trinity. Patrick saw this intimacy as a grace—and it was. But grace builds upon nature. His experience of prayer in the cold nights of Ireland is a tribute, too, to the lessons his parents and the town clergy had tried to instill in him. Something stuck.

In his writings, he expresses piety and affection for each of the divine persons: Father, Son, and Holy Spirit. Chapter 4 of his *Confession* might rightly be called an outburst of love for the Trinity. It's very much like the Apostles' Creed, but it bears an even more striking resemblance, some scholars note, to the writings of St. Victorinus of Pettau.[28] It would be interesting to know how Patrick got to know

---

27. St. Patrick, *Confession*, 16, as quoted in White, pp. 35–36.
28. White, p. 112.

those writings: Did he read them directly, or did he spend time with people who were influenced by them? These are the sorts of things we can only guess about; there are too many blank spaces in Patrick's story for us to fill them in with confidence. As we'll soon see, there are traditions that he spent time training in Gaul—but no hard evidence.

Still, Patrick's creed does tell us what kind of Christian he was. He was a completely orthodox Catholic Christian. However he learned his theology, he learned it well.

So he must have learned some lessons from his parents and priests back home, even if he thought he wasn't paying attention at the time. If nothing else, he had learned how to pray and fast—to call upon the Lord.

And he did call upon the Lord, and the Lord answered him. One night, he heard a clear voice: "You are fasting to good purpose. Soon you will go back and see your homeland again."

CHAPTER 5

The Escape

What did the voice mean? Patrick kept praying, and "after a very short time" he had an answer: "Look! Your ship is ready."

Apparently, the answer came with a vision that showed him the ship and where it was. But it wasn't going to be easy getting there. "And it was not near at hand, but was distant, perhaps two hundred miles," Patrick says. "And I had never been there, nor did I know any one there."[29]

---

29. St. Patrick, *Confession*, 17, as quoted in White, p. 36.

The Fugitive Slave

Two hundred miles! It's true that Patrick was talking about Roman miles, which were only five thousand feet,[30] instead of English miles, which are 5280 feet. But two hundred of them is still a long way to go on foot under the best circumstances. And Patrick wasn't living under the best circumstances. He was a slave, and a slave traveling for two hundred miles had to look over his shoulder every step of the journey. Think of the days of American slavery: the Underground Railroad was a vast organization devoted to helping slaves from the South reach freedom—and even with all that help, most of them never escaped. Patrick would have no such help.

In fact, he might even still have to worry when he arrived home, even if he did make it across two hundred miles of unknown Irish territory and find the ship he had seen in his vision.

Slavery was a condition recognized by law. We could almost say that owning slaves was a recognized human right.

That worked two ways. Of course, Roman slave owners expected that they would have the legal right to keep the slaves they owned. They had paid good money for those slaves.

---

30. The Roman foot was almost the same as the English foot.

But that meant that the slave trader had a right to sell them. Where had he got them? Sometimes, poor citizens sold their infant children to be raised as slaves. But often, slaves were captives. The Roman army might enslave defeated enemies, for example. But slaves were a valuable commodity, and Rome's neighbors found it was a very profitable business to raid lightly defended towns and cart off the inhabitants to be sold. This is what happened to Patrick.

What is surprising to modern minds is that his captors had a recognized right to their property. Patrick became a slave in the eyes of Roman law. It's not too surprising, though, if you think about the implications of slavery. If slavery exists at all, the property right of slave owners has to be recognized. Otherwise, it becomes impossible to keep slaves: the moment the owner's back is turned, the slave will just walk away to some place that doesn't recognize slavery. This was what the Southern plantation owners constantly worried about before the Civil War. It was why they kept pressing for strict enforcement of the Fugitive Slave Act: if a slave could just cross the border into Pennsylvania and be free, then all their investment in human livestock could be worthless overnight.

The historian Roy Flechner tells us that there were certain conditions under which a Roman citizen could be accepted back as a citizen if he had been enslaved by barbarians and then escaped. One of them was if he had been taken willingly or not. If he had put up enough of a fight when the slavers got him, then that was all right. Another was if, when he escaped, he got back home as quickly as he practically could.[31]

These were the things Patrick had to consider when he thought about escaping from slavery. They were weighty considerations. Remember that he had been spending day after day out in the wilderness completely alone for six years, and yet he had never tried to escape. That shows us how daunting the prospect of trying to get away must have been.

But a voice from heaven—that was something to reckon with.

Patrick's Ship Comes In

So Patrick got up and undertook the two-hundred-mile journey to port. It turned out to be an uneventful journey. "And thereupon I shortly took to flight, and left the man with whom I had been for six years, and I came in the

---

31. Flechner, p. 103.

strength of God who prospered my way for good, and I met with nothing to alarm me until I reached that ship."[32]

But that was when things stopped going smoothly.

The incident must have made a vivid record in Patrick's mind, because he tells it with more color and detail than he usually puts into the incidents of his own life.

> And on the very day that I arrived, the ship was leaving its moorings, and I said that I had to sail from there with them. But the shipmaster was annoyed, and replied roughly and angrily, "Don't even *think* of going with us."
>
> When I heard this, I left them to go to the hut where I was staying, and on the way I began to pray. And before I had finished my prayer, I heard one of them shouting loudly after me, "Come quickly! These men are calling you!" And I went back to them right away.
>
> And they started to say to me, "Come on! We're taking you on in good faith. Make friends with us in any way you like." And I refused to suck their breasts, because of the fear of God; but nevertheless I hoped that some of them would come into the faith of Jesus Christ—for they were

---

32. St. Patrick, *Confession*, 17, as quoted in White, p. 36.

> heathen. For that reason I stayed with them, and
> we set sail immediately.[33]

Those curious words "suck their breasts" have suggested to some historians some sort of pagan adoption ritual. But it's more likely that Patrick, whose head was full of Scripture all the time, simply meant to say that he refused to fall in with their pagan ways. He was probably thinking of something like Isaiah 60:16: "And thou shalt suck the milk of the Gentiles, and thou shalt be nursed with the breasts of kings" (in the Douay-Rheims version).[34]

So Patrick boarded a ship full of Irish pagans. It's quite possible that they were pirates like the ones who had abducted him in the first place—although the historian J. B. Bury thinks they were traders[35] who were bringing a cargo of Irish wolfhounds, which in those days seem to have been much in demand among Roman dog-fanciers. After three days of sailing, they reached land.

But where were they? This is another thing Patrick doesn't tell us. He doesn't mention a stormy voyage. He

---

33. St. Patrick, *Confession*, 18, translated by the author from the Latin, *Libri Sancti Patricii* (Dublin: Royal Irish Academy, 1905).
34. Flechner, p. 99.
35. See J. B. Bury, *The Life of St. Patrick and His Place in History* (London: Macmillan & Co., 1905), p. 31.

doesn't tell us anything about the trip at all. But when they got to land, it wasn't a very inviting place.

"And after three days we reached land, and journeyed for twenty-eight days through a desert; and food failed them, and hunger overcame them."[36]

This is not the sort of thing that usually happens if you reach the port you set out for. Where were they?

The Long Walk

The usual explanation is that the ship had reached some part of the northwestern coast of Britain. But another theory is that the ship reached Gaul—modern France. That would account for the three days of sailing. But where in Gaul is there a "desert" that would take a month to walk through?

The historian J. B. Bury suggested that the crew had landed in Gaul just after the devastating barbarian invasions chronicled by historians of the fifth century.[37] The land was deserted because it had been laid waste by the invaders, and the sailors were deliberately avoiding the main highways and towns so as to avoid running into the barbarian hordes.

---

36. St. Patrick, *Confession*, 19, as quoted in White, p. 37.
37. See J. B. Bury, *The Life of St. Patrick and His Place in History* (London: Macmillan & Co., 1905), p. 31.

All this would be more convincing if we knew when Patrick escaped, but once again, we run into the problem that we just don't know any dates for anything that has to do with Patrick. It certainly is true that large parts of Europe were devastated by invasions during his time. We would probably have a hard time imagining just how devastated they were. Whole cities disappeared, and prosperous farming provinces turned into deserts where there was practically nothing to eat.

So we just have to put it down as one more of the things we'll never quite know for sure about Patrick. When he left Ireland, he ended up in Britain, or possibly Gaul, and he had to wander through a wilderness where there was nothing to eat. Even the crew's dogs were fainting from hunger. (In Bury's theory, these would be those Irish wolfhounds the crew was hoping to sell.)

> "Look here, Christian," the captain of the ship said when things had got really desperate. "You say your God is great and all-powerful. So why can't you pray for us? We're likely to starve here! It looks like we might never see a human being again."[38]

Patrick tells us he stood up for his faith.

---

38. St. Patrick, *Confession*, 19, in White. New translation from Latin.

Then I said plainly to them, "Turn in good faith and with all your heart to the Lord my God, for whom nothing is impossible, so that he may send you food right now until you're satisfied—for he has abundance everywhere."[39]

So Patrick led them in prayer, and God came through for them. Suddenly, there was a herd of pigs crossing their path. They caught plenty of pigs, and they had a big pork roast. The men and the dogs ate as much as they wanted.

This made the men think a little differently about Patrick. "And after this they rendered hearty thanks to God," Patrick tells us, "and I became honorable in their eyes; and from that day on they had food in abundance."

But they still weren't converted, or at least not completely converted. For dessert, they found some wild honey. But when one of them offered it to Patrick, the man mentioned, "This is offered in sacrifice." They had made a sacrifice of the honey to one of their pagan gods. Immediately, Patrick thought of what St. Paul said about that.

Eat whatever is sold in the meat market without raising any question on the ground of conscience. . . . But if some one says to you, "This has been offered

---

39. St. Patrick, *Confession*, 19, as quoted in *St. Patrick: His Writings and Life*, p. 37, with minor alterations.

> in sacrifice," then out of consideration for the man who informed you, and for conscience' sake—I mean his conscience, not yours—do not eat it. (1 Cor 10:25–29)

"Thanks be to God," says Patrick, "I tasted none of it."[40]

Patrick's journey naturally made him think of scenes from the Old Testament. Scholars have pointed out how his story resembles Jonah's voyage, for example, and there's no doubt that Patrick tended to put everything in scriptural terms.

In the night after the feast, Patrick had a strange dream—and it reminds us that, for Patrick, events in the spiritual world were even more important than mere physical events like escaping from slavery.

> Now on that same night, when I was sleeping, Satan assailed me mightily, in a way that I shall remember *as long as I am in this body*. And he fell upon me as it were a huge rock, and I had no power over my limbs. But how did it occur to me—to my ignorant mind—to call upon Elijah? And on this I saw the sun rise in the heaven, and while I was shouting "Elijah!" with all my might, lo, the splendour of that sun fell upon me, and

---

40. St. Patrick, *Confession*, 19, as quoted in White, p. 37, with slight modification by the author.

immediately shook all weight from off me. And
I believe that I was helped by Christ my Lord,
and that his Spirit was even then calling aloud
on my behalf.[41]

Some people would have just said it was a bad dream. But Patrick remembered this as one of the most important events of his escape. That shows us something about the way he saw the world. Events on the surface were part of the more important spiritual struggle that had been going on since the world began.

Now Patrick had two problems. He had to find his way back home, but first he had to get away from his companions. It's not clear exactly how they treated him, but something seems to have happened that made them treat him as a captive rather than as a traveling companion. The food lasted for another two weeks; it ran out just as the party finally reached something like civilization. But we can only guess at the story, because the way Patrick tells it is abbreviated and a little confused. Even the math doesn't add up right.

> And, again, after many years, I went into captivity
> once more. And so on that first night I remained

---

41. St. Patrick, *Confession*, 20, as quoted in White, pp. 37–38, with slight modification by the author.

> with them. Now I heard the answer of God saying to me, "For two months thou shalt be with them." And so it came to pass. On the sixtieth night after, the Lord delivered me out of their hands.
>
> Moreover, he provided for us on our journey food and fire and dry quarters every day, until on the fourteenth day we reached human habitations. As I stated above, for twenty-eight days we journeyed through a desert; and on the night on which we reached human habitations, we had in truth no food left.[42]

The historian Roy Flechner wonders whether these numbers are meant to be symbolic, but he admits that it's hard to imagine what they are meant to symbolize. "If they *are* meant to be understood literally," he says, "then we must accept that—holy man though he was—Patrick was simply not very good at maths."[43] On the other hand, Patrick's earliest biographer (writing a long time after Patrick died) interpreted those sixty days as referring to another captivity many years later. Once again, the details are murky, because Patrick is writing to people who don't need details.

---

42. St. Patrick, *Confession*, 21–22, as quoted in White, p. 38.
43. Flechner, p. 101.

Still, the main point of the story of Patrick's escape comes through clearly. Patrick's prayers were answered, and the Lord gave the whole party food, shelter, and fire until they reached civilization.

> And again, after a few years, I was in Britain with my kindred, who received me as a son, and in good faith begged me that at all events now, after the great tribulations which I had undergone, I would not go away from them anywhere.[44]

"After a few years" may mean "since I was captured," or it may mean "since I escaped." Again, we have to remember that Patrick was writing to people who already knew the basic outline of the story, so he didn't have to fill in the details we wish he had filled in. So we come up against another of the great puzzles of Patrick's life. There is a very old tradition that he spent years in Gaul studying with some of the theological greats of the time. Later in his *Confession*, he mentions that he often wanted "to go as far as Gaul in order to visit the brethren and to behold the face of the saints of my Lord—God knows I used to desire it exceedingly"[45]—which suggests that there were people he

---

44. St. Patrick, *Confession*, 23, as quoted in White, p. 38, with slight modification by the author.
45. St. Patrick, *Confession*, 43, as quoted in White, p. 45.

knew in Gaul that he would like to see again. Or it could be that he knew them by reputation and would like to see them for the first time.

Some historians (like J. B. Bury) have thought that Patrick ended up in Gaul after his escape, and stayed there for several years in the monastery at Lérins; the more common story is that he went back home to Britain, and then traveled to Gaul later and spent several years there.

For his part, Patrick skips straight to the next part of the story. Just after telling us that his relatives in Britain begged him to stay, he says,

> And there verily *I saw in the night visions* a man whose name was Victoricus coming as it were from Ireland with countless letters. And he gave me one of them, and I read the beginning of the letter, which was entitled, "The Voice of the Irish"; and while I was reading aloud the beginning of the letter, I thought that at that very moment I heard the voice of them who lived beside the Wood of Foclut which is near the western sea. And thus they cried, as with one mouth: "We beg you, holy youth, to come and walk among us once more."[46]

---

46. St. Patrick, *Confession*, 23, as quoted in White, pp. 38–39, with slight modification by the author.

CHAPTER 6

Preparing for the Mission (Patrick and His Sources)

Back to Ireland? Back to where he had been a slave herding grubby animals out in the wind and rain?

This didn't strike Patrick as his ideal career path. "And I was exceedingly *broken in heart*, and could read no further," he says. "And so I awoke."

But, as he looked back from many years in the future, Patrick could see that God doesn't give up if he has a plan for you. The Irish needed him. "Thanks be to God, that after very many years the Lord granted to them according to their cry."[47]

Dreaming of Ireland

So God kept at it. As Patrick himself tells us,

> I did not proceed to Ireland of my own accord until I was nearly worn out. But this was rather well for me, because thus I was amended by the Lord. And he fitted me, so that I should to-day be something which was once far from me, that I should care for, and be busy about, the salvation of others, whereas then I did not even think about myself.[48]

The way God battered down his resistance was through recurring dreams. Over the next few years, he kept having them—sometimes reassuring, sometimes pleading. Here we notice again that the things of the spiritual world were as real to Patrick as the material world around him—or perhaps even more real.

> And another night, whether within me or beside me, *I cannot tell, God knows*, in most admirable words which I heard and could not understand,

---

47. St. Patrick, *Confession*, 23, as quoted in White, p. 39.
48. St. Patrick, *Confession*, 28, as quoted in White, p. 40.

except that at the end of the prayer he thus affirmed, "He who *laid down his life for you*, he it is who speaks in you." And so I awoke, rejoicing.

And another time I saw him praying within me, and I was as it were within my body; and I heard [someone praying] over me, that is, over *the inner man*; and there he was praying mightily with groanings. And meanwhile I was astonished, and was marvelling and thinking who it could be that was praying within me; but at the end of the prayer he affirmed that he was the Spirit. And so I awoke, and I remembered how the Apostle says, *The Spirit helps us in our weakness; for we do not know how to pray as we ought, but the Spirit himself intercedes for us with sighs too deep for words* (Romans 8:26).[49]

Apparently, these dreams or visions happened over the course of years. At some point, Patrick finally decided he needed to pay attention to them. He would have to go back to Ireland.

His mission, obviously, would be to convert the heathen Irish. But he would not be the first missionary to arrive in Ireland. He wouldn't even be the first bishop.

---

49. St. Patrick, *Confession*, 24–25, as quoted in White, p. 39, with slight modification by the author.

Christians Before Patrick

We saw before how Ireland was on the main Roman trading routes. Christians would certainly have come to the island, and they would have made some converts there. We would know that just by the things that happened elsewhere: there was nowhere in the world accessible to the Romans that Christians did not go, and there was nowhere Christians went where they didn't make at least some converts.

But we happen to know that there were already Christians in Ireland from another important fact. It's a fact that may have confused history quite a bit, and we're not going to be able to sort out the confusion here.

In 431, Pope Celestine sent a bishop *ad Scottos in Christem credentes*[50]—"to the Irish who believe in Christ." This means that there were already Christian communities in Ireland, and the new bishop's first job would be to give them some organization.[51]

This new bishop was named Palladius. According to tradition, he didn't last very long. He arrived and found himself unwelcome. The Irish kings wanted nothing to do with him, and Palladius didn't like the place himself.

---

50. Binchy, 166.
51. Swan, 19–20.

Muirchú, the early Irish biographer of St. Patrick, says that Patrick's consecration as a bishop was delayed because Celestine had sent Palladius to convert the island.

> But God prohibited him; because no one can receive anything from earth unless it were given to him from heaven. For neither did those wild and rough people readily receive his teaching, nor did he himself desire to spend a long time in a land not his own; but he returned to him that sent him. Returning then hence, he crossed the first sea; and, continuing his journey by land, he died in the country of the Britons.[52]

Of course, we have to remember that this biography was written more than two centuries after Palladius and Patrick were dead, so we take its statements for what they're worth. It is certainly true, however, that Palladius was sent to Ireland, because that fact is recorded by the chronicle of Prosper of Aquitaine, who was alive when it happened.

What makes the addition of Palladius to the story so confusing is that, according to one tradition, his given name was also Patricius. If that's true, then there are at least two Patricks in Ireland's early Christian history. Some

---

52. Muirchú moccu Machtheni, *Life of St. Patrick*, 1.8, as quoted in White, p. 77.

modern historians have tried to make Palladius and Patrick the same person, but the great majority of historians have rejected that hypothesis. So we have to deal with two early evangelists in Ireland—one who gave up, and one who refused to give up no matter what.

Patrick himself wasn't happy about the idea of going back to Ireland. But one lesson Christian history has taught us over and over is that the reluctant apostles are the most successful ones.

Getting Ready—with St. Germanus?

It seems that it dawned on Patrick slowly that he was going to have to go back to Ireland. There was a delay of many years, and when he got there, he was a bishop. What happened in all that time? What was he doing to get ready for his mission to the Irish barbarians?

The oldest biographers say that he went to Gaul. Some say he ended up at the famous monastery of Lérins, where he would have met some of the greatest minds in the West at the time.

Muirchú, who wrote the first connected life of St. Patrick, says that when Patrick was thirty years old, he set out for Rome to learn what he could be taught about the sacred mysteries he was going to have to convey to the foreigners.

> And he was thirty years of age, [having grown], as the Apostle says, "into a perfect man, into the measure of the age of the fulness of Christ." He set forth then to visit and pay his respects to the Apostolic See, the head of all the churches of the whole world, as one that was already wise in sacred mysteries to which God had called him, to learn and understand and fulfil them; and that he should preach and impart the grace of God to foreign nations, converting them to the faith of Christ.[53]

But the story says that he never got to Rome, because he met someone who could give him all the training he needed.

> And so he crossed the southern British sea, and began his journey, intending to cross by the Gallic Alps to the furthest point, as he had purposed in his heart; when he found—the choicest gift [of God]—a certain very holy bishop, Germanus, ruling in his city of Alsiodorum.[54]

---

53. Muirchú, 1.5, as quoted in White, p. 76.
54. Muirchú, 1.6, as quoted in White, p. 76.

St. Germanus was bishop of Auxerre in Gaul at a time when Roman authority was falling apart. Like many bishops, he had to take on much of the secular authority abandoned by the incompetent or missing governing powers. He is famous in British history for the Alleluia Victory, which is a story worth hearing—both because it's a great story and because it tells us a lot about the collapse of Roman power that was happening in Patrick's time.

Germanus had been sent to Britain to deal with the Pelagian heresy. Pelagius was a theologian from Britain who preached a radical version of the doctrine of free will. Without going too deeply into it, we can summarize it by saying he believed that human beings could reach heaven without any help from God. Pelagius may have been born in Ireland; St. Jerome, who had a suitable insult for everybody, calls him "really stupid and weighed down with Irish porridge."[55] His teachings became very popular in Britain, but according to the life of St. Germanus—which was written by a man who went with him to Britain—the saint's oratorical powers overcame the opposition.

But Pelagianism was probably not the main thing worrying the British at the time. An unholy alliance of

---

55. *Stolidissimus et Scotorum pultibus praegravatus*. St. Jerome, preface to *Commentary on Jeremiah*.

heathen Picts and Saxons had been wreaking havoc on the island, abandoned for more than a decade by the last Roman legions. There was no force among the ex-Roman British that could stand up to them—except St. Germanus. Having St. Germanus on their side turned out to be better than having a legion. Germanus declared himself the military leader of the Britons, and took a tiny force to ambush the barbarians. He had them lie in wait in a hilly place, and when the barbarians came by the British jumped out of their hiding places and shouted "Alleluia!" as loud as they could. The Picts and Saxons were so frightened by the almighty din that they dropped everything and ran, leaving behind their weapons and plunder.[56] That's how a saint deals with barbarian troubles.

This is the famous bishop who was supposed to have been Patrick's teacher, according to the old stories. But though the stories are old, they are much newer than St. Patrick's time. We can't rely on them as history; we have to put them in that middle ground of possibly true and possibly false. Some historians have insisted that Patrick's language shows that he must have spent time in Gaul; others have found little or no evidence of Gallic influence.

---

56. E. A. Thompson, *Saint Germanus of Auxerre and the End of Roman Britain* (Woodbridge, Suffolk: Boydell Press, 1984), p. 41.

Some find the story of his spending time in Gaul very plausible; others find it very unlikely. Faced with so much uncertainty, we have to shrug and say we don't know.

On the Way to Ireland

At any rate, the story in Muirchú, Patrick's biographer, has it that Patrick set out for Ireland, but not as a bishop, because there was already a bishop—Palladius—for Ireland. But Palladius gave up, and then died shortly after he left, and the news reached Patrick while he was still on his way through Gaul to the coast to leave for Ireland.

> When tidings came of the death of St. Palladius in Britain (because the disciples of Palladius, viz. Augustinus and Benedictus and the rest, returned and told in Ebmoria of his death), Patrick and they who were with him turned aside to a certain famous man, a chief bishop, Amathorex by name, who dwelt in the neighbourhood. And there St. Patrick, knowing the things that were to happen to him, received the episcopal rank from Amathorex, the holy bishop. Moreover, Auxilius and Iserninus and others received lower degrees of the ministry on the same day that Patrick was consecrated.
>
> Then, having received the benedictions, and all things having been accomplished according to

custom (moreover with a special appropriateness to Patrick, this verse of the Psalmist was sung, "Thou art a priest for ever, after the order of Melchizedek"), the venerable traveler got on board, in the name of the Blessed Trinity, a ship prepared for him, and arrived in Britain; and dispensing with everything that could delay his journey [on foot], except what the requirements of ordinary life demand (for no one seeks the Lord by sloth), with all speed and with a favouring wind, he crossed our sea.[57]

If Patrick's biographer is handing down a real tradition, then we notice that Patrick went to Britain first, and from Britain to Ireland. The *Confession* indicates that the British bishops had some authority over Patrick, or at least claimed the right to raise objections to his mission.

So, if Patrick didn't go to Gaul—if the stories that put him at Lérins or with St. Germanus are only legends—then was Britain where he learned to be a bishop?

Trained by Scripture

Some historians have suggested that Patrick could in fact have been trained right in Britain. Britain had a well-established church, and it was capable of producing

57. Muirchú, book 1, chapter 9, as quoted in White, p. 78.

famous theologians. It produced Pelagius, after all, who—whatever Jerome said about him—was an educated man. But this is just speculation.

So if we can't know for certain whether Patrick ever went to Gaul, whether he ever studied with St. Germanus, or whether he was ever at Lérins, then what *can* we know about his training?

Well, we can know what we see all through his writings. He is immersed in Scripture. The Bible is the lens through which he sees everything in the world. He can hardly write a single sentence without dropping in a phrase from Scripture, and he sees biblical parallels in every significant incident of his own life.

What we know about Patrick, and we know it for certain, is that, however he did prepare for his mission, it involved reading Scripture over and over until the words were stamped on his mind in indelible ink. Whether he learned to do that from St. Germanus, or whether he did it in a famous monastery in southern Gaul, or whether he just found the Scriptures and read them himself, he must have spent years reading, memorizing, reciting, and contemplating the Bible.

After that preparation, every thought in his head was filtered through a biblical lens. "In two short letters," says Swan, "he refers to fifty-four books of the Bible."[58]

This doesn't mean he was consciously quoting all the time. His mind was so full of Scripture that he would naturally pull out scriptural phrases to express any idea. He was living in the world of the Bible: he was Moses, he was Paul, he was Jesus. Not that he thought of himself as equal to any of them, but that he was having the same kinds of experiences. "And if my own do not know me, a prophet has no honor in his own country," he writes to the British soldiers of Coroticus.[59] He is quoting from John 4:44: "For Jesus himself testified that a prophet has no honor in his own country." Without putting himself on the same level as Jesus, he can see that he is having the same experience of rejection that Jesus had. The Bible is not a separate universe for him: it is the world he lives in every day.

And as with everything else, the Bible gave him a set phrase to describe where he was headed. He was going to "the end of the earth." (See Is 49:6, Acts 1:8, and many other places.)

---

58. Swan, 63.
59. St. Patrick, "Letter," 11, translated from *Libri Sancti Patricii*.

"The end of the earth" is not just rhetorical hyperbole for Patrick. Ireland is, as far as he knows, the literal end of the earth. It is the farthest habitable point of land. Classical geographers believed that nothing beyond Ireland could support human life.[60] And not only was Ireland at the outer edge of the world, but Patrick spent his years of slavery at the outer edge of Ireland—in the far west, on the edge of the western sea, as far away from home as he could be. "The perception of being on the edge of space could not be greater," says Swan.[61]

That gave Patrick's mission an end-times significance. By preaching the Gospel to the Irish, Patrick was preparing the way for the Second Coming. Just before his ascension, Christ had told his apostles, "[Y]ou shall be my witnesses in Jerusalem and in all Judea and Samaria and to the end of the earth" (Acts 1:8). Patrick was thoroughly convinced that he was living in the last days. His own mission was bringing them about.

This is one of the most important things to understand about Patrick's mission. We can't imagine how important it was to him unless we step into his mind and see that the world is coming to an end. It's not just a good deed

---

60. Swan, 86–87.
61. Swan, 89.

to bring the Gospel to the Irish pagans: it's an emergency rescue mission. This is the last chance for these Irish pagans, and this is the last chance for Patrick himself to be counted among the faithful servants when the Day of the Lord comes.

Fortunately, Patrick had prepared himself well. Not only did he have all of Scripture to draw upon, but he also had the one thing perhaps only his years of slavery could have given him. He had learned how to pray.

CHAPTER 7

Patrick and His Prayer

One thing that strikes us as modern readers is how sure Patrick was that he had been sent by God. He was perfectly aware that he wasn't any great scholar or even particularly virtuous, but he knew that God had chosen him—even if at the beginning he resisted God's choice.

What made him so certain? Partly it was his success. He had made thousands of converts, even though he was, in his mind, a backwoods uneducated hick and a sinner.

But we have the strong impression that Patrick would have insisted that he had been called by God even if he had never made one convert. He just knew. And that was probably because he was in constant communication with the Head Office.

Patrick's habit of prayer began when he was a slave in Ireland, as we've heard before.

> Now, after I came to Ireland, tending flocks was my daily occupation; and constantly I used to pray in the day time. Love of God and the fear of him increased more and more, and faith grew, and the spirit was moved, so that in one day [I would say] as many as a hundred prayers, and at night nearly as many, so that I used to stay even in the woods and on the mountain [to this end]. And before daybreak I used to be roused to prayer, in snow, in frost, in rain; and I felt no hurt; nor was there any sluggishness in me—as I now see, because then *the spirit was fervent* within me.[62]

From then on, we hear that every important turn in his life came after a prayer. The sailors weren't going to let him on the boat that took him away from slavery; Patrick prayed, and they changed their minds. He felt the Spirit praying inside him. "And meanwhile I was astonished, and was marvelling and thinking who it could be that was

---

62. St. Patrick, *Confession*, 16, as quoted in White, pp. 35–36.

praying within me; but at the end of the prayer he affirmed that he was the Spirit."[63]

This is one of the things that make Patrick different. He had a deep relationship with the Trinity in a way that few even among the saints could match.

When Patrick writes his creed in his *Confession*, it may be partly because he had been accused of unorthodox belief. (We don't know exactly what he was accused of, so we can only guess.) But we get the impression that it's a lot more than that. It seems more as though he wrote it because he couldn't help it. He was bursting with love for the Trinity, and it had to come out.

The Creed of St. Patrick

> Because there is no other God, nor was there ever any in times past, nor shall there be hereafter, except God the Father unbegotten, without beginning, from whom all things take their beginning, holding all things [i.e., Almighty], as we say, and his Son Jesus Christ, whom we affirm verily to have always existed with the Father before the creation of the world, with the Father after the manner of a spiritual existence, begotten ineffably before the beginning of anything.

---

63. St. Patrick, *Confession*, 25, as quoted in White, p. 39.

And *by him* were made *things visible and invisible*.

He was made man; and having overcome death, he was received up into heaven to the Father.

And *he gave to him all power above every name of things in heaven and things in earth and things under the earth; and let every tongue confess to him that Jesus Christ is Lord and God* in whom we believe.

And we look for his coming soon to be; he the Judge of the quick and the dead, *who will render to every man according to his deeds*.

And *he shed on us abundantly the Holy Ghost*, the gift and earnest of immortality, who makes those who believe and obey to become *children of God* the Father and *joint heirs with Christ*, whom we confess and adore as one God in the Trinity of the Holy Name.[64]

In its content, St. Patrick's creed is very close to the creeds we recite at Mass, especially the Apostles' Creed. But in its atmosphere, it's very different.

The creeds we recite at Mass are very precise. They're meant to state exactly what we believe, and even more

---

64. St. Patrick, *Confession*, 4, as quoted in White, p. 32.

importantly to exclude certain wrong ideas. Each phrase came about because the Church had to respond to a wrong idea that had actually come up in somebody's theology. As a result, the creeds are a lot like legal documents.

Patrick's creed is different. It has all the same ideas in it, but it hits us like an emotional outburst. He has taken the facts of Catholic theology and made them into a love poem. No one could doubt after reading this that Patrick's theology was orthodox, but more than that, no one could doubt that it was more than mere theology. It was a personal relationship with all three Persons of the Trinity.

This was the unique gift Patrick left his Irish flock. To many—probably most—Catholics, the Trinity is an abstract idea, a product of carefully working out the implications of certain theological truths. To Patrick, the Trinity is a family, and he can't believe how fortunate he is to be adopted into it. This feeling becomes an Irish tradition: we need only remember the story of the shamrock. (We're certainly not going to get through this book without mentioning the shamrock.)

The Lorica

This Trinitarian tradition comes out in a long prayer attributed to St. Patrick. Some historians have made an argument that it actually was composed by him. The majority would say that it was composed later. But it's very much in the spirit of Patrick. It was passed down in Irish for countless generations; its earliest manuscript dates from before 1100. By the 1800s, it had almost passed out of popular tradition; it was still recited only in the backcountry of Ireland. But then, scholars brought it back out from the manuscripts, and with the revival of everything Irish it has become a very popular prayer again. There are some differences between the manuscripts, but not in anything essential.

It's known as the Lorica. A *lorica* is Latin for a breastplate (see 1 Thes 5:8), so metaphorically it's a prayer for protection. In one of the manuscripts that preserve the prayer, there's a preface that tells the story of when and why Patrick wrote it.

> Patrick made this hymn; in the time of Loegaire macNeill it was made, and the cause of its composition was for the protection of himself and his monks against the deadly enemies that lay in ambush for the clerics. And it is a lorica of faith for

the protection of body and soul against demons and men and vices: when any person shall recite it daily with pious meditation on God, demons shall not dare to face him, it shall be a protection to him against all poison and envy; it shall be a guard to him against sudden death, it shall be a lorica for his soul after his decease.

Patrick sang it when the ambushes were laid for him by Loegaire, in order that he should not go to Tara to sow the Faith, so that on that occasion they were seen before those who were lying in ambush as if they were wild deer having behind them a fawn, viz. Benen [Benignus], and "Deer's Cry" [*Faeth Fiada*] is its name.[65]

The story of the deer is one of the many magical legends of St. Patrick: when King Loegaire, or Loiguire, was trying to kill them, Patrick and his companions appeared to change into deer, so that the would-be murderers couldn't find their victims. Incidentally, one of the translators of the Lorica thinks the writer of the manuscript misunderstood the name "Faeth Fiada": it might have been the name of a kind of magic spell. More about that in a moment.

---

65. R. Atkinson, trans., with revisions by Newport J. D. White, as quoted in White, pp. 63–64, with slight modification by the author.

Patrick and His Prayer   77

The prayer is meant to be said every morning, and it starts right off with a resounding invocation of the Trinity.

I

I arise to-day:
in vast might, invocation of the Trinity;
belief in a Threeness;
confession of Oneness;
towards the Creator.

II

I arise to-day:
in the might of Christ's Birth and His Baptism;
in the might of His Crucifixion and Burial;
in the might of His Resurrection and Ascension;
in the might of His Descent to the Judgment of Doom.

III

I arise to-day:
in the might of the order of Cherubim;
in obedience of Angels;
in ministration of Archangels;
in hope of resurrection for the sake of reward;

>   in prayers of Patriarchs;
>   in predictions of Prophets;
>   in preachings of Apostles;
>   in faiths of Confessors;
>   in innocence of holy Virgins;
>   in deeds of righteous men.

IV

>   I arise to-day:
>   in the might of Heaven;
>   brightness of Sun;
>   whiteness of Snow;
>   splendour of Fire;
>   speed of Lightning;
>   swiftness of Wind;
>   depth of Sea;
>   stability of Earth;
>   firmness of Rock.

V

>   I arise to-day:
>   in the might of God for my piloting;
>   Power of God for my upholding;
>   Wisdom of God for my guidance;
>   Eye of God for my foresight;

Ear of God for my hearing;
Word of God for my utterance;
Hand of God for my guardianship;
Path of God for my precedence;
Shield of God for my protection;
Host of God for my salvation;
against snares of demons;
against allurements of vices;
against solicitations of nature;
against every person that wishes me ill far and near;
one or many,

VI

I invoke therefore all these forces:
against every fierce merciless force that may come
upon my body and my soul;
against incantations of false prophets;
against black laws of paganism;
against false laws of heresy;
against encompassment of idolatry;
against spells of women and smiths and druids;
against all knowledge that is forbidden the human soul.

VII

> Christ for my guardianship to-day:
> against poison, against burning,
> against drowning, against wounding,
> that there may come to me a multitude of rewards;
> Christ with me, Christ before me,
> Christ behind me, Christ in me,
> Christ under me, Christ over me,
> Christ to right of me, Christ to left of me,
> Christ in lying down, Christ in sitting, Christ in rising up,
> Christ in the heart of every person, who may think of me!
> Christ in the mouth of everyone, who may speak to me!
> Christ in every eye, which may look on me!
> Christ in every ear, which may hear me!
> I arise to-day:
> in vast might, invocation of the Trinity
> belief in a Threeness;
> confession of Oneness;
> meeting in the Creator;
> Domini est salus, Domini est salus, Christi est salus;
> Salus tua, Domine, sit semper nobiscum.[66]

---

66. Atkinson, trans., as quoted in White, pp. 63-67, as quoted in *St. Patrick: His Writings and Life*, 63–67.

Whether this is Patrick's composition or not, it certainly comes from his tradition. First of all, the strong emphasis on the Trinity was one of Patrick's gifts to Irish Catholic culture. That was one of the things people most remembered about him—again, think of the story of the shamrock. If the prayer was a later composition, we can still understand why Irish monks would have read the first few lines and said, "This must be Patrick's."

It also has a real missionary usefulness. It adapts itself perfectly to the local culture. The Irish were fond of magical incantations, and equally lived in fear of magical incantations. An Irish pagan's world was full of supernatural beings who lived in the twilight just beyond the visible, and who could be persuaded by an incantation to do him a bit of good—or could be persuaded by his enemies to do him harm. So, on the one hand, an Irish pagan had to have incantations ready to help him get through the challenges of the day. And on the other hand, he had to have other ones ready to counter whatever incantations his enemies were using against him.

Incantations work best when they're long and impressive. Like legal documents, they cover every potential case.

So, in this prayer, new Irish Christians got just what they needed. It has all the impressiveness of a really good incantation. It covers all the bases. It asks for everything good and for protection against everything bad. It covers the whole litany of things an Irish Christian who still worries about those invisible powers could be afraid of—"women and smiths and druids," for example. (It may amuse us to note "women" among the things to be feared, but it's easy to imagine how, in a time when political power and violent force weren't open to them, women might be expected to resort to spells to even out the balance of power.)

But at the same time, the prayer is completely Christian. It may adopt the form of a magic spell, but it is an orthodox Christian prayer. And not only is it orthodox, but in fact, it runs through reminders of all the most important facts of orthodox Catholic Christianity. By carefully memorizing it the way they would one of their magic spells, the new Irish Christians were learning the basics of the Catholic Christian Faith.

Patrick himself was quite aware of how powerful these traditional beliefs were. Another legacy of Patrick—and one that he shared with all the best missionaries—was the idea that Christianity works with the local culture.

This was one of his first tenets. And it's worth studying his technique, because—like Patrick—we Catholics are increasingly faced with the problem of evangelizing a culture that doesn't know Christianity and may be actively hostile to it.

CHAPTER 8

Patrick and His Work

When it comes to understanding how Patrick worked, we have less to go on than we might like. We'd really like to know some of his adventures. We can be certain that he had adventures—in a land of a hundred kings, anyone trying to spread the Christian faith must have had some interesting times. Patrick only hints at them, though, telling us that his life was in danger at least a dozen times, but—as usual—assuming that we're not interested in the details.

> Now it were a tedious task to *declare particularly* the whole of my toil, or even partially. I shall briefly say in what manner the most righteous God often delivered me from slavery and from twelve perils whereby my soul was endangered, besides many plots and *things which I am not able to express in words*. Nor shall I weary my readers. But I have as my voucher God who knows all things even before they come to pass, as the answer of God frequently warned me, the poor, unlearned orphan.[67]

We do know that his conversions were not always welcomed by the chiefs and kings. He especially mentions that some of the daughters and sons of the local nobility became Christians, much to the displeasure of their parents.

> Sons and daughters of Irish chieftains are seen to become monks and virgins of Christ. Especially there was one blessed lady of Irish birth, of noble rank, most beautiful, grown up, whom I baptized; and after a few days she came to us for a certain cause. She disclosed to us that she had been warned by an angel of God, and that he counseled her to

---

67. St. Patrick, *Confession*, 35, as quoted in White, p. 42, with slight modification by the author.

> become a virgin of Christ, and live closer to God. Thanks be to God, six days after, most admirably and eagerly she seized on that which all virgins of God do in like manner; not with the consent of their fathers; but they endure persecution and lying reproaches from their kindred; and nevertheless their number increases more and more—and as for those of our race who are born there, we know not the number of them—besides widows and continent persons.[68]

It was not only the nobles who were converted, though. At the other end of the social scale, slaves became Christians, too.

> But the women who are kept in slavery suffer especially; they constantly endure even unto terrors and threats. But the Lord gave grace to many of his handmaidens, for although they are forbidden, they earnestly follow the example [set them].[69]

To Patrick, a slave who becomes a Christian is already set free from the real slavery, which is slavery to sin and death. He knows what St. Paul said about that: "Do you not

---

68. St. Patrick, *Confession*, 41–42, as quoted in White, p. 45, with slight modification by the author.
69. St, Patrick, *Confession*, 42, as quoted in White, p. 45, with slight modification by the author.

know that if you yield yourselves to any one as obedient slaves, you are slaves of the one whom you obey, either of sin, which leads to death, or of obedience, which leads to righteousness?" (Rom 6:16). Patrick, a man who had known literal slavery, is not afraid to take St. Paul at his word. We are all slaves; if we choose to disobey God, we are choosing to obey sin. Sin is a cruel master. "When you were slaves of sin, you were free in regard to righteousness. But then what return did you get from the things of which you are now ashamed? The end of those things is death" (Rom 6:20–21).

The only real freedom is obedience to God, and that means that Christians, no matter what their earthly station, are free. This is the freedom that matters, because it is eternal.[70]

This doesn't mean Patrick had no sympathy for the earthly sufferings of people who were enslaved. As we'll soon see, nothing made him more furious than seeing innocent people forced into slavery. But it does mean that he kept his eternal perspective, even when he was furious.

---

70. Swan, 194.

Spending His Wealth

In order to smooth the way, Patrick sometimes gave out gifts to the local chiefs, and apparently, he hired certain young nobles to be his guides or escorts as he went from one petty kingdom to another. Here again, Patrick gives us a hint of a story without any of the details we'd really like to have.

> On occasion, I used to give presents to the kings, besides the hire that I gave to their sons who accompany me; and nevertheless they seized me with my companions. And on that day they most eagerly desired to kill me; but my time had not yet come. And everything they found with us they plundered, and me myself they bound with irons. And on the fourteenth day the Lord delivered me from their power; and whatever was ours was restored to us for the sake of God and the *near friends* whom we had provided beforehand.[71]

Here Patrick tells us of another captivity, where he was held for two weeks, apparently in spite of having been accompanied by local princes. We can guess that he might have run afoul of some tribal feud, but guessing is all we can do—Patrick doesn't give us details. He mentions

---

71. St. Patrick, *Confession*, 52, as quoted in White, p. 48.

it only to show that evangelizing Ireland has been hard work, and he's put some effort into it.

But he may incidentally have hinted here at what was the cause of the scandal back in Britain that drew this defense from him. He refused to accept gifts, yet he gave generous gifts to kings. Where did he get the stuff? He doesn't say. Yet he spent quite a bit on bribes, to put it bluntly.

> Moreover, you know by proof how much I paid to those who were judges throughout all the districts which I more frequently visited; for I reckon that I distributed to them not less than the price of fifteen men, so that you might enjoy me, and I might ever enjoy you in God. I do not regret it, nor is it enough for me. Still *I spend and will spend more*.[72]

"Judges" may mean people who had judicial power—and thus might hold the fates of new converts in their hands—or tribal leaders, like the judges of Israel in the Book of Judges. Either way, Patrick spent "the price of fifteen men" on gifts for them. It's interesting to see that "men" are the commodities that come to mind to describe the value

---

72. St. Patrick, *Confession*, 53, as quoted in White, pp. 48–49, with slight modification by the author.

of a large sum of money. Slaves were expensive, and no one knew better than Patrick how much they were worth, since he had been one of those commodities himself.

At any rate, it was quite a bit of money, or the equivalent in some other form of wealth. If he refused to accept gifts, where did Patrick get the money? That might have been the question that came up among the British clergy when garbled and incomplete stories of Patrick's work came back to them.

We don't know the answer to that question, but it seems likely that Patrick was spending his inheritance. His father, we remember, was a wealthy landowner who could afford to have many "menservants and maidservants." In the "Letter to the Soldiers of Coroticus," Patrick reminds us of his noble birth:

"I was freeborn according to the flesh; I am born of a father who was a decurion; but I sold my noble rank—I blush not to state it, nor am I sorry—for the profit of others."[73]

"I sold my noble rank" could mean that he converted the land he inherited into portable wealth that could be used to further his mission. That would certainly explain

---

73. St. Patrick, "Letter," 10, as quoted in White, pp. 56–57.

where Patrick got enough money to give gifts to princes and judges.

Unfortunately, we just don't know enough about Patrick's career to be able to answer all our questions completely. We do know enough about Patrick, though, to say that he was both resourceful and honest. He would work with the local culture, and if judges expected gifts, then that was how he would deal with them. But he would not get the gifts in any way that was dishonest, or even in any way that might possibly look dishonest. He was too conscious of his status as a walking billboard for Christianity to make such a mistake in marketing. And the man who wrote the *Confession* was too fundamentally honest to try to get by with anything that his own conscience wouldn't have approved of.

Beyond that, we don't know most of the facts of Patrick's ministry. But there is one incident about which we know some detail.

The Soldiers of Coroticus

After Patrick had been working in Ireland for a while, and apparently making great progress, a British warlord's raiders suddenly attacked.

The circumstances were traumatic for Patrick. His flock had suffered a particularly bloody raid by marauding pirates. The raid coincided with the day of a mass baptism—so, many Irish Christians were killed, Patrick said, while the chrism was still fresh and visible on their foreheads.

It was a mirror image of what had happened to Patrick himself when he was sixteen years old. Instead of Irish slavers killing and capturing Britons, it was British slavers killing and capturing Irish people. Since it happened right after the new converts were baptized, it was probably Easter.

There was one big difference between the Irish raiders who had captured Patrick and the British raiders who, years later, captured Patrick's new converts. Patrick was outraged especially because these pirates were British—and thus were at least nominally Christian.

In his furious state, he sent the pirates a first letter, which they ignored.

On the day following that on which the newly baptized, in white array, were anointed—it was still fragrant on their foreheads while they were cruelly butchered and slaughtered with the sword by the aforesaid persons—I sent a letter with a holy presbyter whom I had taught from his infancy, clergy accompanying him, with a request that they would grant us some of the booty and of the baptized captives whom they had taken. They jeered at them.[74]

Now Patrick was filled with righteous rage, and he wrote another letter. Only this second letter has survived for us to read. He doesn't shrink from condemning the pirates' action, banning them from the sacraments, and reminding them of hell, which they had merited by their murders, thefts, and kidnapping. Even his words seem to tremble with rage as he writes about the events. What was even crueler than the slavers' raid was that they intended to sell the Christian captives to the Picts—who lived as pagans, and in Patrick's eyes notoriously bad ones.

On this account the Church bewails and laments her sons and daughters whom the sword has not as yet slain, but who are banished and carried off

---

74. St. Patrick, "Letter," 3, as quoted in White, pp. 54–55.

> to distant lands where sin openly, grievously, and shamelessly abounds. There freemen are put up for sale, Christians are reduced to slavery, and, worst of all, to most degraded, most vile and apostate Picts.[75]

Patrick had done what could be done for the victims, and they had been taken away anyway. They were across the sea in northern Britain now. So now what? All Patrick could do was muster all the moral authority he had as a Christian bishop and try to reach the Christian souls among Coroticus' followers.

For that reason, Patrick dwells on his episcopal authority in the "Letter"—although he tempers it with his usual modesty. But that makes the authority all the more authoritative: he has authority not because he went after it but because God chose to give it to him.

"Patrick the sinner, truly unlearned:—I confess that I am a bishop, appointed by God, in Ireland. Most surely I deem that from God I have received what I am."[76]

---

75. St. Patrick, "Letter," 15, in White, p. 58.
76. St. Patrick, "Letter," 1, as quoted in White, p. 54, with slight modification by the author.

He also points out that the "Letter" is in his own handwriting, which gives it even greater authority.[77] It's not just instructions from a bishop delivered by usual channels: it's a direct intervention by a bishop.

> With my own hand I have written and composed these words to be given and delivered and sent to the soldiers of Coroticus—I do not say to my fellow-citizens or to the fellow-citizens of the holy Romans, but to those who are fellow-citizens of demons because of their evil deeds.[78]

With this authority, he pronounces Coroticus excommunicated—not only from the church, but from all respectable society.

> For this reason, *holy and humble men of heart*, I beseech you very much. It is not right to pay court to such men, nor to take food or drink with them; nor ought one to accept their almsgivings, until [they do] sore penance with shedding of tears, they make amends to God, and liberate the

---

77. Swan (p. 55) points out that Patrick may have Paul's letters in mind, in several of which Paul adds a few words in his own handwriting to add his personal authority. Compare, for example, Galatians 6:11: "See with what large letters I am writing to you with my own hand."

78. St. Patrick, "Letter," 2, as quoted in White, p. 54, with slight modification by the author.

> servants of God and the baptized handmaidens of Christ, for whom he died and was crucified.[79]

After delivering his threats, he spells out the implications of his ordination. He states emphatically:

> These are not my own words which I have put before you in Latin; they are the words of God, and of the apostles and prophets, who have never lied. "Anyone who believes will be saved; anyone who does not believe will be condemned"—GOD HAS SPOKEN.[80]

Throughout the "Letter" we can feel Patrick's rage boiling. The men and women who had looked to him as a spiritual father had been slaughtered on a holy day—and those were the lucky ones. The survivors were sent to be slaves of the heathen Picts.

Yet Patrick was a Christian through and through. The natural human reaction would be to want revenge. Instead, Patrick hopes for conversion. He ends his letter still furious, but expressing the hope that Coroticus and his men will have a change of heart. This sets Patrick apart

---

79. St. Patrick, "Letter," 7, as quoted in White, pp.55–56, with slight modification by the author.
80. St. Patrick, "Letter," 20, translated from *Libri Sancti Patricii*.

as a saint: his friends have been murdered and enslaved, and he hopes to see the perpetrators in heaven.

> I beseech very much that whatever servant of God be ready, he be the bearer of this letter, that on no account it be suppressed or concealed by any one, but much rather be read in the presence of all the people—yes, in the presence of Coroticus himself—so that perhaps God may inspire them to amend their lives to God sometime; so that even though late they may repent of their impious doings—murderer of the brethren of the Lord!—and may liberate the baptized women captives whom they had taken, so that they may deserve to live to God, and be made whole, both here and in eternity.[81]

As a Christian bishop, Patrick has a duty to souls everywhere. He can't just give way to his anger. He can't even shrug and say the eternal destiny of Coroticus' raiders isn't his problem. "Even though the sinful Christians of Coroticus' soldiers appear to reside outside his episcopal jurisdiction," says Fr. Swan, "his sense of responsibility for their conversion is undiminished."[82]

---

81. St. Patrick, "Letter," 21, as quoted in White, p. 60, with slight modification by the author.
82. Swan, 58.

So how did the story come out? We don't know. As usual with Patrick's life, we don't know the date of the event. We don't know who Coroticus was, either. It seems most likely that he was a warlord in northwestern Britain, on the border of Pictish territory. But British history knows more than one Coroticus.

Once again, the "Letter," which in some ways is full of vivid detail, can't give us any reliable history. We know that the incident happened, but we can't tell how it relates to other things that were going on at the same time.

And once again, the "Letter" gives us a lively portrait of the man who wrote it. Patrick's heart and soul is in it—far more than if he had written in perfect school-approved Latin. So we're fortunate that he had two pieces of bad luck that provoked him to bare his soul. The other one produced the *Confession*.

The Confession

At some point during Patrick's ministry in Ireland, the British bishops evidently heard some accusations against him. We don't know exactly what they were, and they may have been simmering for a long time. Patrick implies in his *Confession* that he has been thinking of writing for quite a while, but something finally pushed him over the edge.

It seems that one of the accusations was that sin, whatever it was, that he had committed when he was fifteen years old. He had confessed it long since to a very dear friend, and apparently that friend betrayed his confidence.

> After the lapse of thirty years *they found*, as an *occasion* against me, a matter which I had confessed before I was a deacon. Because of anxiety, with sorrowful mind, I disclosed to my dearest friend things that I had done in my youth one day, nay, in one hour, because I had not yet overcome.[83]

Patrick admits frankly that he was a sinner at fifteen, and that he did not really believe in God. But God took care of all that. He sent Patrick to Ireland to be a slave for six years.

> But this was rather well for me, because thus I was amended by the Lord. And he fitted me, so that I should to-day be something which was once far from me, that I should care for, and be busy about, the salvation of others, whereas then I did not even think about myself. . . . Wherefore then *I say boldly* that my conscience does not blame me either here or hereafter. God is my

---

83. St. Patrick, *Confession*, 27, as quoted in White, p. 40.

witness that I have not lied in the matters that I have stated to you.[84]

What Patrick cannot understand is why his friend betrayed his confidence. This was a friend who had told Patrick that Patrick would be a bishop, long before Patrick himself thought he would be raised to that dignity. How could he turn around and betray his friend? But Patrick wasn't there at the time, so he doesn't know the whole story. The betrayal happened in Britain when Patrick was in Ireland.

> But rather I am grieved for my dearest friend that we should have merited to hear such an answer as that; a man to whom I had even entrusted my soul! And I ascertained from not a few of the brethren before that contention—it was at a time when I was not present, nor was I in Britain, nor will the story originate with me—that he too had fought for me in my absence. Even he himself had said to me with his own lips, "Behold, you are to be raised to the rank of bishop;" of which I was not worthy. But how did it occur to him afterwards to put me to shame publicly before every one, good and bad, in respect of an [office] which before that

---

84. St. Patrick, *Confession*, 28, 31, as quoted in White, pp. 40-41.

he had of his own accord and gladly conceded [to me], and the Lord too, who is *greater than all*?[85]

At this distance in time, we'll never know what Patrick's sin was, or what his friend's motivation was for revealing it so long after the fact. But we can be grateful for the sin, as Patrick was grateful for his time of slavery. Without the accusations, whatever they were, we never would have had Patrick's *Confession*. Because of that sin, and because of whatever other irregularities he was accused of, Patrick was forced to write. And because he was forced to write, we know Ireland's founding saint from the inside out.

That is a very precious gift.

As for the rest of the story, we'd love to know the details. We'd love to hear the stories of adventure. In a land of a hundred kings, how did all the local royalties receive him? He says his life was in danger a dozen times—what happened then? How did he get out of those scrapes?

There are writers who are very willing to fill in those gaps for us. They may not be telling us the exact historical truth. But they will tell us some very entertaining stories.

---

85. St. Patrick, *Confession*, 32, as quoted in White, p. 41, with slight modification by the author.

CHAPTER 9

The Conversion of Ireland

When we try to figure out what Patrick actually did in Ireland, we run up against a big problem: he was too successful. Ireland became a thoroughly Christian country, and the Irish Christians attributed their conversion to Patrick. He became the great national saint and hero. Because of that, everybody wanted a piece of him. Every tiny village wanted to be able to say that the holy St. Patrick walked down this path and left this footprint. Because of that, it's very hard to tell where Patrick actually went.

Historians who accept the old biographies and chronicles—and those historians are a small minority today—are forced to draw long, squiggly lines that end up touching most of Ireland to show where Patrick went on his long journeys. Most historians have concluded that Patrick's activities were probably confined to the northern part of the island—the part that is Northern Ireland today.

One legend that seems to have some basis is that Patrick was especially associated with the ancient city of Armagh. It may have been his base of operations, and the monastic community there claimed his authority when disputes about precedence came up. Today there is a Roman Catholic Cathedral of St. Patrick in Armagh and a Church of Ireland Cathedral of St. Patrick, making it one of the few places with two cathedrals named after the same saint. (The Church of Ireland is part of the Anglican Communion; it calls itself *catholic*, but it is not in communion with Rome.)

His own writings are little help in telling us where Patrick worked or what specifically he did. But they do give us some information about his general principles— and those principles show us that Patrick owed his success partly to a strong understanding of psychology. In modern terms, he was a good marketer as well as a great saint.

A Policy of Straightforwardness

For example, Patrick made it a habit always to refuse gifts from his converts. He dwells on that at length in the *Confession*, because he was apparently answering accusations that he had profited from his mission.

> *But though I be rude in all things*, nevertheless I have endeavored in some sort to keep myself, both for the Christian brethren, and the virgins of Christ, and the *devout women* who used of their own accord to present me with their little gifts, and would cast of their ornaments upon the altar; and I returned them again to them. And they were scandalized at my doing so. But I did it on account of the hope of immortality, so as to keep myself warily in all things; for this reason, namely, that the heathen might receive me and the ministry of my service on any grounds, and that I should not, even in the smallest matter, give occasion to the unbelievers to defame or disparage.
>
> Perhaps then, when I baptized so many thousands of men, I hoped from any one of them even as much as the half of a scruple. *Tell me and I shall restore it to you*. Or when the Lord ordained clergy everywhere by means of my mediocrity, and I imparted my service to them for nothing, if I

demanded from one of them even the price of my *shoe; tell it against me and I shall restore you* more.[86]

At first, his Irish hosts seem to have been offended by Patrick's refusal of their gifts. But it was very important to Patrick not to give them any reason to suspect that he wanted something material from them. And it seems to have worked. People did trust Patrick: they knew that he wasn't trying to wheedle anything out of them. He was concerned only with their salvation. Patrick emphasizes how much effort he put into not just *being* trustworthy, but also establishing a reputation for being trustworthy.

> Moreover, as regards those heathen amongst whom I dwell, I have kept faith with them, and will keep it. God knows I have *defrauded none* of them, nor do I think of doing it, for the sake of God and his Church. I do not want to raise persecution against them and all of us, and I do not want the name of the Lord to be blasphemed because of me; for it is written, *Woe to the man through whom the name of the Lord is blasphemed* [see Matthew 18:7].[87]

---

86. St. Patrick, *Confession*, 49–50, as quoted in White, pp. 47–48.
87. St. Patrick, *Confession*, 48, as quoted in White, p. 47, with slight modification by the author.

This is probably one of the secrets of Patrick's success in Ireland. He knew that his example—how the Irish thought of him—was as important as the message he preached. It was not enough for him to know in his heart that he was innocent; he had to be a walking advertisement for Christian virtue every hour of the day.

These little glimpses of Patrick's work are all we have that we can count on as real history—but they are substantial glimpses. We know his methods. We know his teachings, because he gives us a completely orthodox creed. We know that he was succeeding in converting Irish people of every rank, including not a few princes and princesses. We know that he spent his own fortune freely to smooth the way, often giving gifts to local officials and hiring aristocrats' sons to be his guides as he traveled from one place to the next. And we know that, in spite of his precautions, his life was often in danger—at least twelve times, he tells us. We don't know dates, and that annoys historians. But we do know Patrick.

For any other information, we have to turn to the biographies and chronicles that mention Patrick. But here we are on much shakier ground. The chronicles were written down long after the events, and some historians find evidence that the entries mentioning Patrick were filled in by later chroniclers who were trying to reconcile the Patrick legends with their lists of dates for other events. And the earliest surviving biography about Patrick was written at least two centuries after he died.

The Patrick of Legend

By the time the earliest biographies about St. Patrick appear, legends have already grown up and crusted like barnacles on the saint's life. His story has suffered a sea change into something rich and strange.

Yet these legends are history themselves. They tell us what St. Patrick meant to the generations who came after him. Looking back from an Ireland that was thoroughly Christianized, they saw St. Patrick as nothing less than the founder of their people. He was the Moses of Ireland.

The legends take this identification with Moses to the extreme of making Patrick live to be 120 years old, the same age Moses was when he died. Now, it isn't absolutely impossible for a human being to live to that age—the oldest recorded human being in modern times is a woman in Paris who lived to be 122. But it's very unlikely. This is one of the reasons some historians have accepted the idea of multiple Patricks: it's easier to account for the long life span if there was more than one man living it.

But the life span is not the important part of the parallel with Moses. Moses led his people out of slavery to the heathen Egyptians, and Patrick led his people out of slavery to the heathen Irish pagan religion.

In our modern enlightened age, most Catholics would say that paganism was simply a delusion. The Christian religion is true; the pagan religion is false, in the simple sense that it does not correspond to reality. The pagan gods are imaginary beings; they have no more power in the real world than Superman or Mighty Mouse.

For Patrick's biographers, though, the pagan religion was "false" in a different sense. It had real power, but its power came from the devil. It was demonic. Its power was for the purpose of leading its followers to hell.

The Old Testament Book of Exodus has the same attitude toward the pagan religion of the Egyptians. Pharaoh's magicians have real power. The first few times Moses tries to demonstrate the power of God, Pharaoh's magicians are able to duplicate his miracles with their trickery. For example, Moses tells his brother Aaron to throw down his rod, and it will become a serpent.

> So Moses and Aaron went to Pharaoh and did as the LORD commanded; Aaron cast down his rod before Pharaoh and his servants, and it became a

serpent. Then Pharaoh summoned the wise men and the sorcerers; and they also, the magicians of Egypt, did the same by their secret arts. For every man cast down his rod, and they became serpents. But Aaron's rod swallowed up their rods. Still Pharaoh's heart was hardened... (Ex 7:10–13)

Two more times, the magicians manage to duplicate Moses' miracles.

Moses and Aaron did as the LORD commanded; in the sight of Pharaoh and in the sight of his servants, he lifted up the rod and struck the water that was in the Nile, and all the water that was in the Nile turned to blood. And the fish in the Nile died; and the Nile became foul, so that the Egyptians could not drink water from the Nile; and there was blood throughout all the land of Egypt. But the magicians of Egypt did the same by their secret arts; so Pharaoh's heart remained hardened... (Exodus 7:20–22)

So Aaron stretched out his hand over the waters of Egypt; and the frogs came up and covered the land of Egypt. But the magicians did the same by their secret arts, and brought frogs upon the land of Egypt. (Exodus 8:6–7)

Only when the plague of gnats comes do the magicians confess themselves stumped.

> Aaron stretched out his hand with his rod, and struck the dust of the earth, and there came gnats on man and beast; all the dust of the earth became gnats throughout all the land of Egypt. The magicians tried by their secret arts to bring forth gnats, but they could not. So there were gnats on man and beast. And the magicians said to Pharaoh, "This is the finger of God." (Exodus 8:17–19)

It didn't help, of course: Pharaoh was still stubborn.

The contest with Pharoah's magicians shows us something of how the Israelites viewed the Egyptians' false religion: it had real power. It was tempting precisely because it was powerful. And that was how the early Christians tended to view pagan religion. It is true that some Christians saw it as simply false, in the modern sense of being imaginary. But for many, the pagan gods were powerful demons who could be summoned by a magician and made to perform convincing tricks.

The *Acts of Peter*, one of the many apocryphal books that circulated among some early Christians but were not accepted as canonical Scripture, tells the story of a long contest between St. Peter and Simon Magus, the magician mentioned in the Acts of the Apostles "who had previously practiced magic in the city and amazed the nation of Samaria, saying that he himself was somebody great" (Acts 8:9). In the Acts of the Apostles, Simon believes in Christ and is baptized, but he tries to buy Peter's power to work miracles—thus giving his name to the sin of *simony*, the buying and selling of spiritual goods. When Peter tells him to repent, Simon asks Peter to pray for him, and that's the last we hear of him in the Bible. But in the legends gathered in the Acts of Peter, Simon sets himself up as an anti-Christian prophet, claiming to be "the power of God," and performs miracles almost as impressive as the ones Peter can show. He comes to his end when he shows off by flying into the air, and Peter brings him crashing down to earth with a prayer. Even then, the fall doesn't kill Simon; he dies (very realistically) from the incompetence of the surgeons who try to patch him up.

These stories about Peter were told for the same reason similar stories would be told about Patrick: Christians saw Peter as a new Moses, leading his Church out of slavery to sin and death. He faced powerful opposition, not only among the earthly authorities but also from the demonic forces.

As we've already seen, the first full biography of St. Patrick is by Muirchú moccu Machtheni, usually just called Muirchú, who wrote it just before the year 700—probably more than two hundred years after Patrick died. Some of his information comes from Patrick's own writings, but he adds a lot of other details that Patrick did not mention. Some of them are plausible; some are clearly legendary. But the legends have a consistent point of view. They portray Patrick as the victorious warrior against ancient Irish paganism. And, just as with Pharaoh's magicians, the Irish magicians have real power.

In fact, they have the power to see just how dangerous Patrick is to them. Muirchú tells us that there was a high king named Loiguire son of Neill (or Loegaire MacNeill), and his pagan clergy informed him that their whole way of life was in danger.

The End of Heathenism Prophesied

> Now he had about him wise men and magicians and augurs and enchanters and inventors of every evil art, who through their heathenish and idolatrous religion had skill to know and foresee all things before they came to pass. And of these there were two who were preferred beyond the others, whose names were, Lothroch, otherwise

Lochru, and Lucetmael, otherwise Ronal. And these two by their magical arts frequently foretold the coming of a certain foreign religion, in the manner of a kingdom, with a certain strange and harmful doctrine, brought from a long distance across the seas, proclaimed by a few, accepted by the many, and honoured by all; one that would overturn kingdoms, slay kings that resist it, lead away multitudes, destroy all their gods, and, having cast down all the resources of their art, reign for ever and ever.

Moreover they indicated him who should bear and advocate this religion. And they prophesied in the following words cast into poetical form, words frequently uttered by them, more especially in the two or three years which preceded the coming of Patrick. Now these are the words of the poem, which are somewhat obscure, on account of the idiom of the language.

"Adze-head will come

With his crook-headed staff,

And his house [chasuble] holed for his head.

He will chant impiety from his table in the east of his house.

His whole household will respond to him. So be it, So be it."

> Which can be more plainly expressed in our language. When therefore all these things come to pass, our kingdom, which is a heathen one, will not stand.
>
> And so it afterwards came to pass. For the worship of idols having been overturned on the coming of Patrick, the faith of Christ—our Catholic faith—filled the whole land.[88]

The "obscure" poem is plain enough in its main meaning. Patrick wears a hat like an adze, the mark of a Christian bishop. He carries a crook-headed staff. The "house holed for his head" is the chasuble he wears. The table in the east of his house is the Christian altar, traditionally placed in the east of the church, and the "impiety" is the Mass. And the whole congregation responds "Amen"—"So be it."

Did the pagan priests of Ireland really predict the coming of Christianity?

Well, it wouldn't have been hard to see coming. Remember that Ireland had had trading links with the Roman Empire for centuries. The island was at the edge of the world, but it was not uninformed. Everyone would have known that the Roman Empire was Christian, and

---

88. Muirchú, 1.10, as quoted in White, p. 79.

everyone would have known that the Christians were keen on spreading their religion. Muirchú portrays the magicians' prophecy as an example of their demonic powers, but any moderately clever observer would have seen that Christian missionaries would be coming sooner or later. Seeing what had happened in other nations on the borders of the Roman Empire, the pagan priests might well have tried to warn their king that bad things would happen if he let those Christians come in and run amok. The poem itself may be a much later legend, but it probably portrays a real truth about the encounter of paganism with Christianity in Ireland: the pagans knew what was coming, and it had them worried.

Back to His Old Master

When Patrick did come, according to Muirchú, he meant to go back to his old master and buy his freedom. This may show us the ambiguous attitude to slavery among the Irish of Muirchú's time. If it was legitimate to own slaves, then Patrick's running away from his master—whose name, according to the story, was Miliucc—was a kind of theft. He was Miliucc's property. Only by paying his own price could Patrick get that theft off his conscience; only if the story showed him trying to pay that price could the Irish really believe he was a righteous man.

But it's also very consistent with what Patrick tells us about his own methods. He was careful to make sure he didn't owe anybody anything. Whatever obligations secular society seemed to impose on him, he was eager to make sure he fulfilled them. We can easily imagine that his escape would weigh on his own conscience, no matter how unjust his enslavement had been. But we can even more easily imagine him deciding that it would be good policy to buy his freedom, so that the Irish he was trying to convert would not be able to raise that objection.

At any rate, the way Muirchú tells the story, Patrick had been hoping not only to pay off his old master, but also to convert him. But it didn't quite go the way he planned.

> And when here, it seemed to him that there was nothing better for him to do than to ransom himself in the first instance. So he sought thence the north country, carrying a twofold ransom from slavery—that is, an earthly and a heavenly—to that heathen man Miliucc, in whose house he had once lived in captivity, that he might deliver from captivity him whom he had formerly served as a captive....

Now when Miliucc heard that his slave was coming to see him, to the end that he should, at the close of his life, adopt, as it were by force, a religion which he disliked, [fearing] lest he should be in subjection to a slave, and that he [the slave] should lord it over him, he committed himself to the flames, at the instigation of the devil and of his own accord. Having collected around him every article of his property, he was burnt up in the house in which he had lived as king.

Now St. Patrick was standing in the aforesaid place on the southern side of Mount Mis, where, coming with such gracious purpose, he first caught sight of the country where he had been a slave, a spot which is now marked by a cross; and at the first view of that country, there, under his eyes, he beheld the burning pyre of the king.

And so, stupefied at this deed, he spoke not a word for two or three hours. And then with sighs and tears and groans he uttered these words, and said, I know not; God knows. As for this king man who hath committed himself to the flames, lest he should become a believer at the close of his life, and serve the everlasting God—I know not; God knows;—none of his sons shall sit as king upon the throne of his kingdom from generation to generation; moreover his seed shall be in servitude for evermore."[89]

This strange story at first strikes us as very implausible. There's no evidence other than the story itself that it is true, but it may not be as implausible as it sounds. We don't know enough about Patrick's progress to know where this story fits in it. But he does seem to have made allies of local kings; we certainly know that he converted a number of Irish aristocrats. If Patrick was a lone missionary, it would seem absurd that his wealthy master would commit suicide rather than even talk to him. But if he was already at the head of a movement that was gaining traction everywhere, he might have looked like a steamroller coming toward Miliucc. A stubborn pagan surrounded by newly Christianized rivals might have seen no alternative but conversion or death. An aristocrat might find it simply unthinkable to subject himself to his slave in any way; even in Rome, where it was common for slaves to buy their freedom, the stigma of having been a slave lasted for generations.

Once again, there's no evidence that this story is true history. What it does tell us for certain is what the

---

89. Muirchú, 1.11–12, as quoted in White, pp. 80–82, with slight modification by the author.

people of Muirchú's time thought. They saw Patrick as the winning side in a titanic battle. They saw Irish paganism as a powerful but doomed force, and they saw it fighting Patrick with its last breath. That much of the story is almost certainly true. Paganism was powerful, and it did fight, and it was doomed. Patrick won.

The battle between paganism and Christianity soon takes a very familiar form. Patrick faces off against King Loiguire's magicians, just as Moses had faced off against Pharaoh's magicians.

First there was the magician Lochru. Muirchú says that he "had the audacity with swelling words to disparage the Catholic faith." He continues,

> As he uttered such things, Saint Patrick regarded him with a stern glance, as Peter once looked on Simon; and powerfully, with a loud voice, he confidently addressed the Lord and said, O Lord, who can do all things, and in whose power all things hold together, and who hast sent me here—as for this impious man who blasphemes your name, let him now be taken up out of this and die speedily. And when he had thus spoken, the magician was caught up into the air, and then let fall from above, and, his skull striking on a

rock, he was dashed to pieces and killed before their faces; and the heathen folk were dismayed.[90]

Here, Muirchú explicitly brings up the legend of Simon Magus and his contest with St. Peter. But in the events of the next day, we are reminded even more of Moses and Pharaoh.

Battle with the Magician Lucetmael

Now while all were feasting, the magician Lucetmael, who had taken part in the contest at night, was eager, even that day when his comrade was dead, to contend with St. Patrick. And, to make a beginning of the matter, he put, while the others were looking, something from his own vessel into Patrick's cup, to see what he would do. St. Patrick, perceiving the kind of trial intended, blessed his cup in the sight of all; and, lo, the liquor was turned into ice. And when he had turned the vessel upside down, that drop only fell out which the magician had put into it. And he blessed his cup again, and the liquor was restored to its own nature; and all marvelled. . .

---

90. Muirchú, 1.17, as quoted in White, p. 86, with slight modification by the author.

And after the cup, the magician said, "Let us work miracles on this great plain."

And Patrick answered and said, "What miracles?"

And the magician said, "Let us bring snow upon the earth."

Then said Patrick, "I do not wish to bring things that are contrary to the will of God."

And the magician said, "I shall bring it in the sight of all."

Then he began his magical incantations, and brought down snow over the whole plain to the depth of a man's waist; and all saw it and marveled.

And St. Patrick said, "Well, we see this thing; now take it away."

And he said, "I cannot take it away till this time tomorrow."

And the Saint said, "You can do evil, but not good. I am not of that sort."

Then he blessed the whole plain round about; and the snow vanished quicker than a word could be spoken, without any rain or cloud or wind. And the multitude shouted aloud, and marvelled greatly.

And a little after this, the magician invoked his demons, and brought upon the earth a very thick darkness, as a miracle; and all murmured at it.

And the Saint said, "Drive away the darkness."

But he could not in this case either.

St. Patrick however prayed and uttered a blessing, and suddenly the darkness was driven away, and the sun shone forth. And all shouted aloud and gave thanks.

Now when all these things had been done by the magician and Patrick, in the sight of the king, the king said to them, "Throw your books into water, and we shall worship him whose books come out unharmed."

Patrick replied, "I will do it."

But the magician said, "I do not wish to enter into a trial by water with this fellow; for water is his God." He had evidently heard of baptism by water given by Patrick.

And the king answered and said, "Throw them into fire."

And Patrick said, "I am ready."

But the magician, being unwilling, said, "This man worships as his God water and fire in turns every alternate year."

And the Saint said, "That is not so; but you yourself shall go, and one of my lads shall go with you, into a house separated and shut up; and my garment shall be around you, and your garment around me, and thus shall you together be set on fire; and ye shall be judged in the sight of the Most High.

And this suggestion was adopted; and a house was built for them, whereof one half was built of green wood and the other half of dry. And the magician was put into the part of the house made of green wood; and one of Saint Patrick's lads, named Benineus, was put with a magician's robe into the part that was made of dry wood. The house was then shut up from the outside, and set on fire before the whole multitude. And it came to pass in that hour, that as Patrick prayed, the flame of the fire burnt up the magician with the half of the house that was made of green wood, the cloak of Saint Patrick only remaining whole, inasmuch as the fire did not touch it. Benineus, on the other hand, was fortunate with the half of the house that was made of dry wood; for, as it is told about the Three Children [see Daniel 3], the fire did not touch him at all; nor was he alarmed, nor did it do him any harm; only the cloak of the magician which was around him was, by the will of God, burnt up.

And the king was greatly enraged against Patrick, because of the death of his magician, and he almost rushed upon him, minding to slay him; but God hindered him. For at the prayer of Patrick and at his cry, the wrath of God fell upon the ungodly people, and many of them perished. And St. Patrick said to the king, "Unless you believe now, you shall die speedily, because the wrath of God will fall upon your head." And the king feared exceedingly, "and his heart was moved," and his whole city with him.[91]

Now, did all that really happen? Our rational twenty-first century minds rebel against the idea of magic snowfalls and trials by fire. But we shouldn't completely dismiss stories like this one. The legends and miracle stories may not tell us the actual history of St. Patrick, but—once again—they are history. They tell us what people believed and how they thought.

It's important to remember that, because it's easy for us to become too rationalistic about the stories of St. Patrick. We're tempted to think that, because the events

---

91. Muirchú, 1.20, as quoted in White, pp. 89–91, with slight modification by the author.

they describe probably never happened, the stories are worthless. That would be a mistake. What they tell us is what Patrick became to the Irish people. He was their Moses. He was the victory of Christian truth over pagan superstition. The contest with the magician Lucetmael may not have happened, but it represents the truth in a memorable way. The truth is that paganism was a very powerful force, but Patrick's Catholic Christianity overcame it.

We can get an idea of how tradition worked on the facts of history by seeing how Muirchú treats one of the stories we happen to know as a fact: the story of Coroticus and his raid.

> I will not pass over in silence a certain wonderful deed of Patrick's. The vile action of a certain British king named Coroticus, a wretched cruel tyrant, was reported to him. Now this man was the greatest possible persecutor and slayer of Christians. Patrick, however, endeavored by a letter to recall him to the way of truth; but he mocked at his salutary warnings. When, however, this was reported to Patrick, he prayed to the Lord and said, "O God, if it be possible, banish this faithless man both from this world and the world to come."

No long time had elapsed when he caused a magical spell to be chanted before him, from which he heard that in a brief space he would pass away from the royal throne. And all the men dearest to him broke out into language of the same purport. He then, when he was in the midst of his court, took on the spot the form of a little fox—a pitiable object—and departed in the presence of his friends; and from that day and that hour, like flowing water that passes away, he was never seen again.[92]

We know that there is a kernel of historical truth here. There was a king named Coroticus, and he did slay Christians, and Patrick did write a letter that he intended to be read in Coroticus' presence. There's no contemporary record of what happened after that, so we don't know whether Coroticus really changed into a little fox. We're probably safe in saying that it's not likely.

If we had only the story from Muirchú to go by, we might think of this as just a miracle legend with no basis in history. Because we know that this one did have a historical basis, though, we might suspect that some of the other

---

92. Muirchú, 1.29, as quoted in White, pp. 100–101, with slight modification by the author.

stories in Muirchú also began as real historical facts. We just can't tell exactly where fact ends and legend begins.

Muirchú's version of the Coroticus story does give us one hint about how the stories changed as history passed into legend. Look at Patrick's prayer. "When, however, this was reported to Patrick, he prayed to the Lord and said, 'O God, if it be possible, banish this faithless man both from this world and the world to come.'"

The Patrick of the legends is quick with a curse. We saw that in the story of his old master, whom he pronounced condemned to hell for all eternity. In this one case, though, we know the *real* Patrick's reaction. In the middle of his fury, when Patrick's human nature must have been wishing to see Coroticus burn in hell for all eternity, here is what he actually wrote: he asked the bearer of the "Letter" to make sure it was

> read in the presence of all the people—yes, in the presence of Coroticus himself—so that perhaps God may inspire them to amend their lives to God sometime; so that even though late they may repent of their impious doings—murderer of the brethren of the Lord!—and may liberate the baptized women captives whom they had taken,

so that they may deserve to live to God, and be made whole, both here and in eternity.[93]

This is the real Patrick. In spite of his fury—which is boiling over even as he writes these words—he still hopes that Coroticus can be saved. His human instincts may want to see Coroticus in hell, but Patrick is a saint. His prayer is that he will see Coroticus in heaven.

This is the extreme case. This is Patrick at his most furious, when he has just seen his friends murdered—and yet he prays for the conversion of the murderers. If that was how Patrick reacted to the raid of Coroticus, we can be sure he was never quick to pronounce a curse. The later legends have been filtered through minds that were sincerely Christian, but not quite so saintly.

That, unfortunately, is what every evangelist will have to leave behind. The very great evangelists, like Patrick, can leave behind a nation of Christians. No one can make a nation of saints. But Jesus doesn't expect a nation of saints. "Those who are well have no need of a physician, but those who are sick; I have not come to call the righteous, but sinners to repentance" (Lk 5:31-32).

---

93. St. Patrick, "Letter," 21, as quoted in White, p. 60, with slight modification by the author.

So Patrick didn't make the Irish perfect. They still had a hundred kings, all fighting each other. They were still superstitious, like every human culture, and they still didn't love their neighbors as themselves.

But they were trying.

And for sinners like us, St. Patrick has left quite a legacy.

CHAPTER 10

Patrick and His Legacy

It's St. Patrick's Day, and everything is green. In the United States, people are drinking green beer. Wherever there are Irish people, there are people celebrating. Wherever there aren't Irish people, there are people pretending to be Irish. Shamrocks are everywhere. Google has one in its logo.

We had to bring up the tale of the shamrock eventually. The story tells us that Patrick used the three leaflets of a clover to illustrate the idea of the Trinity: three distinct parts make up one being. We don't know how old this story is, but there is no ancient record of it. The earliest written account of Irish people using shamrocks to celebrate St. Patrick's Day comes from the 1600s—but it's mentioned there as an established tradition. The first written account of the tradition that Patrick used the shamrock as a symbol of the Trinity comes from the 1700s—but again, that account mentions it as a tradition. There's no way to guess how old the folk tradition really is.

For the botanists out there, the shamrock in Ireland is usually a species of clover, though sometimes it refers to a wood sorrel. In the United States, the plants sold as shamrocks for St. Patrick's Day are almost always wood sorrels (Oxalis species).

Of course, you don't have to be a botanist to appreciate the symbolism of three leaflets making up one leaf. The important thing is that Ireland identifies itself with Trinitarian theology, and the Irish attribute that Trinitarian tradition to St. Patrick. Even if Patrick himself never plucked a shamrock leaf, he was certainly devoted to the Trinity, and he would be pleased that his disciples had learned their lesson from him so well. A whole nation so devoted to the Trinity that it puts shamrocks on the tails of its airliners! Wouldn't Patrick be happy about that? Has any other evangelist succeeded so well?

Patrick couldn't make the Irish perfect, because he wasn't perfect himself. But how he changed Ireland! And then how Ireland changed the history of the Church! Some people say that those Irish Christians should get all the credit for saving civilization as the world grew dark.

We know from Patrick's own writing that some of his converts were taking vows to consecrate themselves to Christ. He was making new monks and nuns in his own lifetime, and the movement only grew after him. Ireland became a nation of monasteries. And as Western Europe collapsed into the Dark Ages, those monasteries preserved Western civilization when it was dying out everywhere else. When it was time for a revival of learning, as the Middle Ages got under way, the Irish were there waiting. Monks from Ireland fanned out over Europe and brought the learning they had preserved, and the manuscripts they had copied.

Ireland itself has had a famously difficult history. Conquered by the English, it was a second-rate colony of a Protestant power for hundreds of years. And the English did everything they could to bury Catholicism and turn the Irish into good, enlightened Protestants. But the Irish weren't having it. No matter how difficult it was to be Catholic, the Irish Catholics persisted. The ones who emigrated from Ireland took their Catholic Faith with them. St. Patrick taught them his persistence.

Today, St. Patrick still has a lot to teach us.

For one thing, we could learn a lot about eschatology from him. *Eschatology* is the study of the end times—the last things. St. Patrick was convinced that the end of the world was near, and that he was helping to bring it closer.

Now, in a limited way, we could say that he was wrong. After all, we're here, more than a millennium and a half after he died, and the world hasn't ended.

But from a saner perspective, we should realize that the end of the world is near. Each one of us is going to die, and much sooner than in a millennium and a half. This short human lifetime—even 120 years is hardly any time when you compare it to all of history—is all we have, and a lot of it has gone by already. At the end of it, we'll have made all our decisions and completed all our accomplishments. What account will we give to the Judge on the day of judgment?

What St. Patrick can teach us is to have that always in mind. We have to live our lives as if the end is near—because it is. Whatever we need to do, tomorrow may be too late.

Patrick can also teach us to remain alert to the Spirit working in us, even when we don't expect it. Have you been having a bad day? Fine—Patrick was kidnapped and sold as a slave and ended up on a windy hill with a bunch of sheep for six years. That's what you call a bad day. But Patrick saw God working in that very bad day to bring a very good result: the conversion of Ireland. We could learn that perspective from Patrick.

Another thing Patrick can teach us is his charity. He could get furiously angry, but he never gave up on anybody. Think of Coroticus and his soldiers: they had murdered and enslaved his friends—and Patrick hoped to lead the murderers to heaven! Most of us nurse grudges, and most of us haven't seen our friends murdered and kidnapped. If Patrick could hope to do good to the murderers, we can get over our petty grudges.

I won't say, "finally," because I don't think I'll ever run out of lessons we can learn from St. Patrick. But here's the last one I'll mention: we can learn to appreciate Scripture. We can learn from Patrick to see that the Bible really is a treasury of all human experience, and that there's always something in Scripture to help us understand the things that happen in our own lives.

These are just some of the things St. Patrick has taught me, and he did it in only two short letters.

Sources

Binchy, D. A. "Patrick and His Biographers Ancient and Modern." *Studia Hibernica* 2 (1962): 7–173.

Bury, J. B. *The Life of St. Patrick and His Place in History*. New York: Macmillan, 1905.

De Vinné, Daniel. *History of the Irish Primitive Church: Together with the Life of St. Patrick, and His Confession in Latin, with a Parallel Translation*. New York: Francis Hart and Company, 1870.

Flechner, Roy. *Saint Patrick Retold: The Legend and History of Ireland's Patron Saint*. Princeton: Princeton University Press, 2019.

Gildas Sapiens and Nennius. *The Works of Gildas and Nennius*. Translated by J. A. Giles. London: James Bohn, 1841.

Hanson, R. P. C. *Saint Patrick: His Origins and Career*. Oxford: Clarendon Press, 1968.

Healy, John. *The Life and Writings of St. Patrick*. Dublin: M. H. Gill & Son, 1905.

Hodgkin, Thomas. *The Visigothic Invasion*. Oxford: Clarendon Press, 1892.

Jackson, Kenneth Hurlstone. *Language and History in Early Britain: A Chronological Survey of the Brittonic Languages, First to Twelfth Century A.D.* Edinburgh: University Press, 1953.

James, Montague Rhodes, trans. *The Apocryphal New Testament*. Oxford: Clarendon Press, 1924.

St. Jerome. Preface to *Commentary on Jeremiah*. In Nicene and Post-Nicene Fathers, Series II, Vol. 6.

Lynch, Paul. "'Ego Patricius, Peccator Rusticissimus': The Rhetoric of St. Patrick of Ireland." *Rhetoric Review* 27, no. 2 (2008): 111–130.

Muirchú. *Life of St. Patrick*. In *St. Patrick: His Writings and Life*, edited and translated by Newport J. D. White, 68–109. London: Society for Promoting Christian Knowledge, 1920.

Procopius. *History of the Wars*. Translated by H. B. Dewing. Cambridge, MA: Harvard University Press, 1914.

St. Patrick. *Confessions*. In *St. Patrick: His Writings and Life*, ed. and trans. Newport J. D. White, 29–51. London: Society for Promoting Christian Knowledge, 1920.

———. "Letter to Coroticus." In *St. Patrick: His Writings and Life*, ed. and trans. Newport J. D. White, 52–60. London: Society for Promoting Christian Knowledge, 1920.

———. *Libri Sancti Patricii*. Dublin: Royal Irish Academy, 1905.

———. *The Works of St. Patrick*. Translated by Ludwig Bieler. New York and Mahwah, NJ: Paulist Press, 1953.

Swan, William Declan. "The Experience of God in the Writings of St. Patrick: Reworking a Faith Received." PhD diss., Pontificia Università Gregoriana, 2012.

Tacitus, Cornelius. *The Works of Tacitus*. Translated by Thomas Gordon. London: J. and F. Rivington, 1770.

Thomas, Charles. *Britain and Ireland in Early Christian Times, AD 400–800*. London: Thames and Hudson, 1971.

Thompson, E. A. *Saint Germanus of Auxerre and the End of Roman Britain*. Woodbridge, Suffolk: Boydell Press, 1984.

———. "St. Patrick and Coroticus." *Journal of Theological Studies* 31, no. 1 (April 1980): 12–27.

Walden, Garrett. "Saint Patrick and His Eschatological Motivation for Missions." Academia.edu. Accessed January 27, 2023.

White, Newport J. D., ed. *St. Patrick: His Writings and Life*. Translated by Newport J. D. White. London: Society for Promoting Christian Knowledge, 1920.

Zosimus. *New History*. In *The History of Count Zosimus*. London: J. Davis, 1814.